eXtreme encounters

start each day on the edge

eXtreme for Jesus

THOMAS NELSON PUBLISHERS

Nashville

Introduction

Today is the beginning of an *extreme* year. As you read through this daily walk with God, you will begin to experience Him in ways you never dreamed of. Jesus said that He came into your life to give you more—more life, better life, *extreme* life.

As you read through these pages, you'll find verses that are your sword against all the things the Enemy throws at you. Read them. Read the stuff under them, then read the verses again. Memorize them if it seems good to you. Remember that you have to keep these things in your heart in order to fight with the Enemy of this world. Don't be content to just read the words on the page and close the book. Get proactive. Read, write, memorize, and share. Tell a friend about what you read. Give them some of the insight you got. Spread the wealth. So, are you ready for the ride? Then turn the page and get started.

Extreme Encounters Subject Index

V

Contributors

Leslie Cunningham is a college student pursuing her master's degree in Speech and Communications. She is a leader of a Disciple Now group and a mentor for high school girls at Green Acres Baptist Church in Tyler, Texas.

Stephen Felts is the founding pastor of Music City Metro Bible Study in Nashville, Tennessee. He currently ministers to young adults and singles at The People's Church in Franklin, Tennessee. He is a national award-winning editor and the author of *Start a Revolution*.

Jeremy and **Nicole Hindman** minister to teens in Richmond, Virginia. Both are pursuing full-time ministry in church reconciliation.

Justin Lookadoo is a national youth speaker and drug enforcement officer for Smith County, Texas.

Scott Mauck is the Student Ministries Pastor at River Valley Community Church and serves as adjunct faculty at Western Seminary in Portland, Oregon.

Hayley Morgan is a national youth speaker and the Brand Manager of "Extreme for Jesus" for Thomas Nelson Publishers in Nashville, Tennessee.

Chris Paluzi is a youth retreat speaker and Campus Crusade for Christ leader. He currently works with Big Brothers/Big Sisters of Middle Tennessee.

Troy Putney is the director of the learning center at a college preparatory school in Brentwood, Tennessee. He has his master's degree in counseling psychology and works with at-risk students.

Mark Smeby is currently the Senior Editor of the Music Channel at the Christian Internet portal Crosswalk.com. in Franklin, Tennessee. He assisted Audio Adrenaline in writing *30 Days with Jesus.*

Brandon Watson is a former youth minister who currently serves as administrator and Bible teacher at The Brook Hill School in Tyler, Texas.

Credits

> I acknowledged my sin to You . . . and You forgave the iniquity of my sin.
>
> **Psalm 32:5**

How do you get forgiveness for your sins? Have you ever been asked that? 'Cause lots of people would love to be forgiven. What do we tell them? "There is none for you; you've gone too far!" Or, "Just get on your knees and beg God for mercy." Wrong! Remember, Jesus died to take away every sin you've ever committed, are committing, or ever will commit. So what do *we* do? One word—*confess*. Admit it. Tell Him you messed up, and then thank Him for the forgiveness that is already ours. See how easy? There is no groveling, no public flogging—just a confession, an acknowledgement of our sin. Don't forget to confess your stuff to God every day.

EXTREME FOR JESUS

"I will lead them in paths they have not known. I will make darkness light before them, and crooked places straight. These things I will do for them, and not forsake them."
Isaiah 42:16

There you are. Skating down the hill. Picking up speed. Your form is perfect. The adrenaline is pumping. Man, you are reaching the most extreme ride of your life. Then, stick in the road . . . skates in the air . . . body flipping . . . *blur*. . . . If only someone would've been going in front of you to make your path safe. That's what God does. If you are relying on Him, seeking to know Him, He will make your crooked paths straight. Sure, there will be obstacles. Obstacles add spice to skating. They also add spice to life. But God has promised that if you focus on Him, He will make your way so that you will not fall.

God, who is rich in mercy, because of His great love with which He loved us, even when we were dead in trespasses, made us alive together with Christ (by grace you have been saved).

Ephesians 2:4–5

It's a hot summer day. You're dying of thirst, so you run down to the convenience store. You get yourself an ice-cold drink and head to the counter. "$1.35 please." You dig into your pocket to pull out one dollar and a quarter, some lint, a rubber band. Yikes! No more money. You're just 10 cents away. But just when you are about to leave, the clerk says, "That's OK; I have a dime." Wow! She didn't have to do that. Something for nothing! That's grace—getting what you don't deserve. Who can you show grace to today? Look for a chance to share this kind of grace with others.

Thursday

Have you ever been to the point of saying, "I am not helping anyone else—ever! No one cares or ever even thanks me!"? You feel that you give and give, and no gratitude is ever expressed. Meanwhile, you watch lots of people do far less and get recognized more. It's not fair. They just help to get the recognition and that is it. Their heart isn't in it. Well, that doesn't give us the excuse to quit. We impact people when we give. We only impact ourselves when we want recognition. Give more.

"All these out of their abundance have put in offerings for God, but she out of her poverty put in all the livelihood that she had."

Luke 21:4

Love . . . does not rejoice in iniquity, but rejoices in the truth; bears all things, believes all things, hopes all things, en-dures all things. Love never fails.

1 Corinthians 13:4-8

Do your batteries ever run out of juice? Are there times when you just can't love anymore? It's at this point that God wants to help. We get so confused because we think love is a feeling. If you don't feel love then you can't act love. But it's a decision, a choice—which means some-times it might not even feel good. The next time your love tank is empty, pull into the filling station of God's Word. Learn what love is from God's point of view. It doesn't have to feel a cer-tain way, but God says that it does *act* a certain way.

EXTREME FOR JESUS

As many as received Him, to them He gave the right to become children of God.

John 1:12

Did you know that you are a child of God? Think about that for a moment. You are God's kid! How much responsibility does that lay on you? How much authority, power, and ability does that give you? There is nothing stopping you from acting like Jesus—except you! When you finally stand in front of God, do you want Him to say, "Who are you?" or do you want to hear, "You are *My kid* and I'm pleased with you!"? With great power comes greater responsibility. Act like a kid of God!

> "Ask, and it will be given to you; seek, and you will find."
>
> Matthew 7:7

Have you ever made any kind of a list? A list of what you want to get done, what you want to do when you grow up, what to get at the store? Lists help us to focus. They help us to organize our thoughts and to concentrate on what it is we really want. Have you ever made a list of what you want most from God? I don't mean a list of goodies, like a new stereo or pair of shoes, but what you want in relationship with Him. Give it some thought. Do you want to know Him more? Do you want peace? Do you need love? Do you want acceptance or appreciation? Make a list of three things you really want from God and pray about those every day this week.

If a friend was walking straight toward a cliff, would you say something to stop them, or would you just let them fall off? Of course you would say something. Right? If you didn't, what kind of a friend . . . scratch that . . . what kind of person would you be? Your unsaved friends are walking toward hell, which is a lot worse than falling off a cliff. What is holding you back from telling them about Jesus? Pride? Fear of rejection? Or is it that you just plain don't care? If you really love them, take the time to share the extreme life of Jesus with them, regardless if you think they'll flip or not.

> Faithful are the wounds of a friend.
>
> **Proverbs 27:6**

> If I say, "My foot slips," Your mercy, O LORD, will hold me up.
>
> Psalm 94:18

Steve and a friend were playing and climbing hills in Steve's jacked-up 4x4 truck. They lined up the truck for one last ride, gave it the gas, and all four wheels started working, grabbing, climbing. They were almost to the top when the dirt under the back tire slipped. The truck flipped upside down and rolled down the hill. All of this because the back tire slipped. When you're pushing life to the edge and living for Christ, there will be times when you feel like you're slipping. But God won't let you. Give it to Him and He'll hold you up.

Repay no one evil for evil.
Romans 12:17

Is there anyone today who you would love to get even with? Anyone who deserves to be taught a lesson? What are your plans? To make them feel your pain? They're expecting it, you know. So why not shock them and give them what they don't expect? Kindness. Compassion. Love. What's more important? Your saving face or your relationship with God? If you answer "God," then find a way to turn the other cheek. Lay on the kindness rather than the grief. Trust God to handle the rest.

EXTREME FOR JESUS

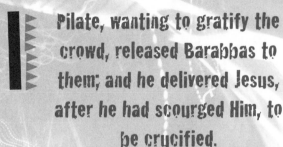

> Pilate, wanting to gratify the
> crowd, released Barabbas to
> them; and he delivered Jesus,
> after he had scourged Him, to
> be crucified.
>
> Mark 15:15

Your friends just handed you a water balloon filled with red dye, and they want you to throw it on the freshman that will walk down the hall any minute. In your heart you know it is wrong, but your friends are counting on you. This will be hilarious. You play many scenarios in your head: I could accidentally drop the balloon. I could throw it at my friends. Or I could just say no. . . . You see the freshman coming and, not wanting to let your friends down, you throw it—knowing that what you're doing is wrong. Do something radical: Stand for what is right instead.

The night has been perfect. Your guy has been a dream. You are sitting in his car. He kisses you good night, then all of a sudden . . . he's all over you. You are trying to block all the shots. But, is it OK? You think that maybe you are being too old-fashioned. No way. This guy just doesn't get it. He is not respecting you, and he for-real isn't following the Bible. So guys and girls, remember: Don't touch it if it ain't yours, and keep your hands to yourself.

> Concerning the things of which you wrote to me: It is good for a man not to touch a woman.
>
> 1 Corinthians 7:1

One thing I do, forgetting those things which are behind and reaching forward to those things which are ahead, I press toward the goal for the prize of the upward call of God in Christ Jesus.

Philippians 3:13-14

Have you done something you know you shouldn't have? Something that was all the way wrong and now you feel guilty? Stop. That's right; stop feeling guilty. If you have fessed up, told God you were wrong, and accepted His forgiveness, then you have nothing else to think about. It's done. Over. Finished. Move and quit reliving it. Paul had to. Imagine if you had murder on your conscience. Talk about guilt. But he chose to forget it and move on. You probably have done wrong, but reliving it in guilt doesn't help anybody. Accept God's forgiveness today, and move on to the dream to win the prize He has offered you.

> Be angry, and do not sin.
> Meditate within your heart
> on your bed, and be still.
> **Psalm 4:4**

Have you ever gotten ticked off? I mean really mad! So mad that your insides started jumping around and your heart started pounding. Jesus did. All of these idiots set up shops in the temple and turned it into a flea market. Jesus threw a fit. He was turning over tables and throwing people out (see John 2:13–16).

Anger is not wrong. But what anger makes us do can be wrong. The Bible warns us to be careful that, in our anger, we do not sin. But some things should make us mad: whacked-out kids shooting up school; little children getting abused; drug dealers selling destruction; old people being put into homes and forgotten. Take that anger and use it to fuel positive action. What really ticks you off? How can you use that emotion to make things better?

EXTREME FOR JESUS

> "Honor your father and your
> mother, that your days may be
> long upon the land which the
> LORD your God is giving you."

Exodus 20:12

Did you know that out of all of the Ten Commandments, this is the only one that has a promise? That must mean it is very important to God. Sometimes honoring your parents seems like the hardest thing you could do. They can sometimes be so clueless, so controlling. But this verse does not say to honor them if they're totally cool. Nope; it says to honor them . . . *period.* If you feel like it or not. If they are Christians or not. If they get it or not. Are you honoring your parents? Do you control your tongue when they say stupid stuff? Do you accept their discipline and guidance? God gave them to you to teach you something. Don't be too blind to see it.

Thursday

They say you don't know what you've got 'til it's gone. Imagine how you would feel if someone you loved was gone. Close your eyes. Sit back and imagine it. Go ahead. . . . Now respond to that feeling today while the people you love are still here. Thank God and share yourself with them. Share God's love with them, too. How can you let them know God loves them today?

> Oh, give thanks to the LORD! Call upon His name; make known His deeds among the peoples!
>
> Psalm 105:1

"Choose for yourselves this day whom you will serve . . . . but as for me and my house, we will serve the LORD."

Joshua 24:15

Every day we live we realize that life is nothing but a series of choices that we have the opportunity to make. Some choices we make are better than others, but we still control our ability to make them no matter how hard they may be. Whether to go to school or skip for the day—it's a choice that we make, so we must *own* those choices. In addition, every choice has a consequence— some good, some better, some not so good. What choices do you face today and which way will you choose?

EXTREME FOR JESUS

"I will give them one heart, and I will put a new spirit within them, and take the stony heart out of their flesh, and give them a heart of flesh."

Ezekiel 11:19

Trying to understand how to have a changed life may seem like a totally complicated thing. There's a simplicity to it, though, that God would love for you to know. He loves you so much just the way you are. But He's pretty clear on the fact that He wants to be the only one you serve—not your grades, your popularity, your friends, or even your family. He wants you to see your sinful nature and admit your need for Him as the only way to salvation. He wants to be served as the only God in your life. When that is true, you'll get a brand-new heart—a new perspective, a new way of looking at life. Have you experienced a changed life?

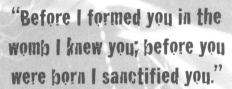

> "Before I formed you in the womb I knew you; before you were born I sanctified you."

Jeremiah 1:5

Eternally loved cherished creation of the Almighty God—that's what you are! He made no mistakes on you. He's never regretted making you. He is so proud of you, nothing could ever change His mind about the way He feels. Long before your mom heard your first cry, God had planned a wonderful life just for you. He knew what great things He wanted you to do for Him before the doctor told your mother she was going to have a baby! God has a specific purpose for you that no other person on the earth can fulfill. He chose that purpose with you in mind. Don't ever think you're not important, special, or loved by God. He has been loving and watching over you since before you came on the scene. If God were asked to describe one of His most treasured possessions, He would describe you.

Tuesday

You can fly in an airplane to 6,000 feet above the earth with a parachute strapped to your back. You can say that you have faith that the parachute will work. But it is a dead faith. Only when you jump out of the plane does your faith come alive. And what a rush! In life, you can say you have faith that God will take care of you. But only when you let go and try something that only God can help you do will your faith come alive. And what a rush!

> Faith by itself, if it does not have works, is dead.
>
> James 2:17

"Because you are lukewarm, and neither cold nor hot, I will vomit you out of My mouth."

Revelation 3:16

How would you like to be someone who makes God want to throw up? Well, that's what you are if your faith isn't hot or cold. If there's nothing about your faith that's extreme, then you're hurting God more than you're helping Him. When you get food poisoning, your body throws up in order to get rid of the toxins. A toxin is a poison that has an evil influence on your health or moral purity. Do you want to be a poison to God? An evil influence causing others to stumble? If your faith has been lukewarm, it's not too late to change. Learn what pleases God. As you spend time in His presence, you will feel the heat and your faith will go to extremes.

It happened one evening that David arose from his bed and walked on the roof of the king's house. And from the roof he saw a woman bathing, and the woman was very beautiful to behold. . . . Then David sent messengers, and took her; and she came to him, and he lay with her.

2 Samuel 11:2, 4

Someone may ask, "Where can sexual lust lead?" That's kind of like asking, "Where can lighting matches lead?" If you play with fire, you're going to get burned. Lust of any kind is the ultimate form of selfishness. You look at something and want it so bad you'll do anything to get it. That's just what David did! Even though every pore in your body wakes up when you're around someone, it doesn't mean that you have to have that person; it just means that you're alive. You don't have to act on your feelings. Choose to identify the selfishness in your passions, and ask God to help you get rid of any thoughts that treat another person without the respect they deserve.

You, O LORD, are a shield
for me.

Psalm 3:3

As Alyson and I began walking back to the missionary house deep inside the ghetto, we found ourselves being followed by a man who was asking us all kinds of questions. Between our vague answers, both of us were crying out prayers of protection in our hearts. We began to walk faster as another guy came out of nowhere and joined in the pursuit. As we turned into the driveway of the mission home, both guys jumped back as though they'd hit a wall. They said that if we were going to the "church home," they were getting out of there. At that point I experienced the power of the shield of God. It has the power to repel whatever enemies come your way. Has the Lord shielded you lately? How?

In Bible days, if you killed an unborn baby then you would be killed, too. Scriptures make no distinction between killing an unborn person and any other person. This is because God tells us that from the moment of conception we are His kids. Maybe you know a girl considering abortion. Encourage her to seek counsel, to find another way to take care of herself without killing her child. God assures us that He will never give us more than we can bear. He will honor her decision, and in the end she will not have to live with the guilt.

"If men fight, and hurt a woman with child. . . . if any harm follows, then you shall give life for life."

Exodus 21:22-23

Let every soul be subject to the governing authorities. For there is no authority except from God.

Romans 13:1

Sometimes it's a drag having parents and teachers forever telling you what to do. They may not always be right, but that's no reason to blow them off. God is the One who brought them into your life. While you may feel your parents and teachers are so out of tune with your life, you can know for sure that God isn't! He knows you better than you know yourself. So He knows what you need better than even you do. Trust His judgment. He really does know what He's doing. Take a moment to thank God for caring enough about you to put people of authority in your life.

EXTREME FOR JESUS

You are a chosen generation, a royal priesthood, a holy nation, His own special people, that you may proclaim the praises of Him who called you out of darkness into His marvelous light.

1 Peter 2:9

Popular question: "What is happening to our youth?" So what is happening, youth? OK, so some of you were raised in broken homes, your dad was never there for you, your uncle molested you. You're so fed up and misunderstood! Who will take away your pain? The better question is: When will you be a conqueror and not a victim? When will you stop blaming everyone else for your behavior? You are chosen. You are the one with a destiny. You are a world changer, a person set apart for a specific purpose. Shout it out about God. You've been called out of the mess of sin. Rise up and conquer!

> In the beginning God created
> the heavens and the earth.
> Genesis 1:1

A group of scientists decided that humans no longer needed God. So they sent a representative to Him. He walked up boldly to God and said, "God, we are advanced and don't need You! We have discovered the secret of life." God smiled and said, "Is that so? Prove it." The scientist grinned and picked up a pile of dirt from the ground. He began working to create life. God shook His finger at the scientist and, with a thundering voice, stated, "No, no. You get your *own* dirt!" If you ever start to think you don't need God, think again.

Have you ever cheated? Ever talked about someone? Have you ever forgotten about God? Have you ever done *anything* wrong? The Bible says we have all sinned, so I know your answer has to be yes. This verse says that men having sex with other men is wrong

> "You shall not lie with a male as with a woman. It is an abomination."
>
> Leviticus 18:22

in the eyes of God. It is a sin. Maybe you know some guys like this. Do you judge them because their sin seems worse than yours? Well stop. All have sinned. Just because theirs seems more obvious than yours doesn't make theirs worse. God loves the homosexual in spite of his sin, just as He loves you.

You will keep him in perfect peace, whose mind is stayed on You, because he trusts in You.

Isaiah 26:3

Inside your head is a VCR. You can choose to play any movie on your VCR that you want. It can be the re-run of the bad fight you had last night with your mom. Or it can be the adventure movie that you believe your life will be. You can go to the video store of your mind and take out any flick you want. You can watch the time your favorite pet died, over and over. Or you can watch the story of how much God loves you. Your VCR. Your movie choice. What will you repeat in your mind? Will it be the good or the bad? You are what you think. So you choose. Will you be a total drag, or two thumbs up?

EXTREME FOR JESUS

"You have heard that it was said to those of old, 'You shall not murder, and who-ever murders will be in danger of the judgment.' But I say to you that whoever is angry with his brother with-out a cause shall be in danger of the judgment."

Matthew 5:21-22

"Sometimes he makes me so mad!" And it's all his fault, isn't it? You may think they *try* to make you mad. It's normal to get frustrated and mad, but imagine what other people think about you when you get ticked. Do they think, *Ah, what a sweet person,* or *What a selfish jerk!*? Do you walk around with anger written all over your face? God wants you to see the danger of always being mad. To Him it's as bad as murder. Be careful that you don't "murder" others with the anger you carry around in your heart.

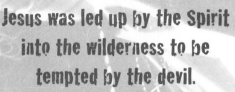

> Jesus was led up by the Spirit
> into the wilderness to be
> tempted by the devil.

Matthew 4:1

We're all tempted daily. We're tempted to do things we shouldn't do. We're tempted to cheat at school. We're tempted to say ugly, angry words to people. We're tempted to hurt others to make ourselves feel better. Well, Jesus was tempted, too. When the devil was standing in front of Him, Jesus could've given in. But instead He decided to fight. And He fought with the only weapon He needed—the Word of God. Today Satan will tempt you. Will you decide to use God's Word as your weapon?

Do you ever feel lonely? Isolated? A school superintendent was asked to give one main reason for the recent school shootings. She answered, "Isolation." Satan's favorite weapon. Divide and conquer. When a lion goes after his prey, he cuts off a single animal from the herd. The whole herd is too strong. But a single deer, alone, is easy to conquer. Satan wants to isolate you so you feel like no one cares. Look at your life. Surround yourself with Christian friends who care about you. Get involved at church and school. Then look at other students you know in your school. Those who seem to be alone. The outcasts. Let them know they're not alone. Ask them to eat lunch with you. Give them a ride. Invite them to church. Don't let Satan divide and conquer.

> Two are better than one. . . . For if they fall, one will lift up his companion.
>
> Ecclesiastes 4:9-10

Jonathan said to David, "Go in peace, since we have both sworn in the name of the LORD, saying, 'May the LORD be between you and me, and between your descendants and my descendants, forever.'"

1 Samuel 20:42

Breaking up is hard to do. Especially when it's your best friend. It feels like you're torn apart. Jonathan and David were best friends who had to say good-bye. Saying good-bye hurts. When you're hurting because of a breakup—whether by moving away, death, or whatever reason—know that it is OK to hurt. Also know that God is still in control. He had a reason for you to have this relationship. He will also use the breakup. Turn to the Father and let Him comfort you. Cry, yell, and tell Him it hurts—all the while watching to see what God wants you to learn through the hurt.

"Do not be afraid. Stand still, and see the salvation of the LORD, which He will accomplish for you today."

Exodus 14:13

Is there a situation in your life you're afraid of? One that you fear will get the best of you. What will you do? Panic? Plan an escape? Seek revenge? So many choices, yet only one is right—stand. "Huh? Stand? How can I do that?" If you trust God, you have to trust that He'll do what He says. And He says that He will fight for us. It's a relief actually, because it takes the pressure off. If you owned a pit bull and a guy was attacking you, would you fight or would you sic your pit bull on him? You have a God who can conquer anything, so next time let Him do the fighting while you stand firm.

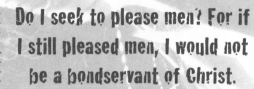

> Do I seek to please men? For if
> I still pleased men, I would not
> be a bondservant of Christ.
>
> Galatians 1:10

A re you a people-pleaser? You dress to impress, you say all the right things, you hang
out in all the right places? Have you ever mea-
sured the stress that causes? "Will he notice
me? Will she like me? Will they leave me?" You
are forever questioning. Wondering. Working.
Would you like relief? Then change your focus.
God isn't so fickle. He's made it clear. He does-
n't change the rules. He doesn't drop you for
offending Him or for dressing weird. If you turn
your focus to pleasing Him, you will find that
all that other stress diminishes. You no longer
need others' approval because you have the
only approval you need. Who are you trying to
impress? If it isn't God, then forget it.

Have you ever tried to climb slowly down a muddy hill? Not so easy, huh? As you step down you can go slow at first, but then look out! The physical side of a relationship is much like that slippery slope. Once you've kissed, you'll never go back to just holding hands. Once you've started to explore each other's body, you'll never go back to just kissing. Get the picture? If solid boundaries are not set early in the relationship, you'll end up in sexual immorality, without even thinking about it. How do you keep from slippin' down the hill? Set your boundaries early in a relationship, and get a friend to hold you accountable.

> Do not stir up nor awaken love until it pleases.
>
> Song of Solomon 2:7

"You shall love the LORD your God with all your heart, with all your soul, and with all your mind."

Matthew 22:37

How would you feel if your crush only talked to you once or twice a week? Or what if you put a love note in their locker, and they never even bothered to read it? Would you feel like they really loved you? So how do you think God feels when we get so busy or lazy that we don't even take the time to talk to Him or read His love letter called the Bible? If we say that we really love God, our actions should reflect it. Walk the talk. If your crush treated you the way you treat God, would you stay with them?

EXTREME FOR JESUS

"I will sing to the LORD, for He has triumphed gloriously!"

Exodus 15:1

Music is an awesome way to express your thanks to God. It's such an emotional rush to combine words of praise with the mysterious power of melody. It can take you away from the concerns and cares of the moment to places of peace, joy, and celebration. Music is so spiritual, and it allows such an intimate expression of our feelings. God made music for His glory, but the world uses this incredible tool to promote its own messages. What messages are you allowing into your spirit through your choice of music? Would God be pleased?

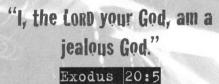

> "I, the LORD your God, am a
> jealous God."
>
> Exodus 20:5

What are you trying to prove? Whose attention do you want to get? If it's anybody's but God's, then look out. He's a jealous God. Yes, jealous. That means you belong to Him, and it makes Him jealous when you act like you belong to someone else. When you try so hard to impress another person. You worry over how much you will be accepted. You scheme over how to be hip. And God gets jealous. "If only you spent that much time trying to impress Me," He whispers. But you're too busy trying to impress someone else. What can you do to impress God? What can you change to keep Him from getting jealous? Do you go places without Him? Use His name in a bad way? Forget you belong to Him? Don't make God jealous.

Thursday

Do you live behind a wall? Have you built a nice barrier between yourself and the rest of the world? I know, it seems safe. You feel like you have to protect yourself. So you put up some bricks and mortar to keep the bad people out. There

> Woe to him who is alone when he falls, for he has no one to help him up.
>
> Ecclesiastes 4:10

you live in your safe little world, untouched by anybody else. Right? Wrong. Walls don't protect you from the world. In fact, they only make things worse. You cannot protect yourself from pain. The only thing the walls keep out is love. God has made us to live in community with one another. In community we find love, peace, happiness, and, yes, even pain. Hide from the pain and you hide from love. Let God tear down your walls. Live with no fear.

When He had removed him, He raised up for them David as king, to whom also He gave testimony and said, "I have found David the son of Jesse, a man after My own heart, who will do all My will."

Acts 13:22

David was a screwup! He was a liar, a murderer, an adulterer, and a thief. So how could God say that David was "a man after My own heart"? It's because David understood the grace of God. He begged for forgiveness, accepted it, and moved on. He allowed God to turn his life around, and his focus became knowing God more deeply. Listen, you *will* screw up, but God loves you and wants to forgive you. Tell Him you sinned. Ask Him for forgiveness. Then accept His love and forgiveness and move on.

EXTREME FOR JESUS

"I am the door. If anyone enters by Me, he will be saved."
John 10:9

You log on to the Internet. You want to
gain access to the mystical World Wide
Web. "Access Denied." What? Oh, you for-
got to type in your password. The only way
that you're allowed to jump on the superhighway is for your user name and login
password to match up. Same with heaven.
Admit to God that you aren't perfect, that
you mess up. Accept the fact that Jesus is
God's Son, and make Him the ruler of your
life. Then you will have God's "password"
stamped on your heart. Then when you log
off in this world, and you're standing before your Creator trying to gain access to
that heavenly superhighway, He will see
that you have been given access through Jesus. Without Jesus as your Lord . . . access
denied!

> **Take up the whole armor of God, that you may be able to withstand in the evil day, and having done all, to stand.**
>
> Ephesians 6:13

Playing laser tag can be lots of fun if you know the course and all the tricks. Anyone who's ever played laser tag knows that you don't want to wear white or bright clothes because you play under black lights, which make you look like a bright moving target. Not a good move!

The same is true in our spiritual life. We don't want to face the battles of everyday life and its struggles in the wrong clothing. We need God's protection and His truth. So surround yourself with God's truth, righteousness, peace, faith, salvation, Word, and prayer! Don't be a bright, moving target for Satan!

Have you ever been in a race and come to "the wall"—that point where you feel as if you have no more to give? Your tank is dry and you're out of gas. We usually have this happen when we run alone. We have no one to push us or encourage us beyond what our capabilities are. When trying to minister to others, it's much easier to do it with others. They encourage us to push down that wall, to make a difference. The flip side is to think of how encouraging you are to others.

> Let us run with endurance the race that is set before us.
>
> **Hebrews 12:1**

"Where two or three are gathered together in My name, I am there in the midst of them."

Matthew 18:20

The power of prayer is truly an awesome thing. It can heal, deliver, and bring peace and comfort. And when we pray with other believers in unity, all having the desire for the same result, it's as though Jesus is standing right in the middle of us! That's what the Bible says. When you pray with your friends, think about Jesus right there with you making what you pray happen. Take advantage of opportunities to join other Christians in prayer. It may not be the coolest thing in the world to some people, but hey, it is one party that Jesus is truly the life of.

EXTREME FOR JESUS

I am full, having received . . .
the things sent from you, a
sweet-smelling aroma, an
acceptable sacrifice, well
pleasing to God.
Philippians 4:18

Remember when you were a kid and
you drew stuff—stick figures, the sun,
stars, houses, stuff like that? Could it go
into an art museum? Did strangers ooh and
aah over it? Did your parents stick it on
the fridge? They probably told you how
beautiful it was and even acted like they
knew *what* it was.

What you give to God may seem unimag-
inative, or even too simple. But is it? What
you give Him is so special that He wants to
"hang it on the fridge." He loves the things
you make for Him, the things you do for
Him. He is so proud of you. So don't ever
think you don't have enough to give God.
Even when your gift to Him seems uncre-
ative, and when nobody else knows what it
is, He loves it, because you are His kid.

> **Then David danced before the Lord with all his might.**
>
> 2 Samuel 6:14

Diamonds are buried deep inside of rocks. Seems like such a beautiful and valuable thing for God to hide under a rock. But it's not the only thing hidden under rocks. "What else?" you ask. Worship. Think of worship like a diamond under a rock. The rock is your will. You can choose to lift the rock to release the worship, or you can choose to sit still under the pressure and not move an inch. If you feel like you just can't let yourself go in front of everyone, that's OK. God doesn't expect everyone to worship Him in the same way. But He's buried the desire to worship under the rock of your free will. It's your choice how and in what ways you will express your worship to Him.

When animals are trained to do tricks, they are rewarded with a special treat that re-inforces the good behavior. God has given us a similar "treat." When we obey Him, He gives us a sense of peace and contentment. You know that feeling you get when you do the right thing? That's a gift from God meant to give you encouragement. Not that God views us as trained animals, but still— if we obey His commands, good things happen. Many people spend their whole lives searching for a sense of peace. In what area does God want to offer you His peace in exchange for your obedience?

> "Whether it is pleasing or displeasing, we will obey the voice of the LORD our God to whom we send you, that it may be well with us when we obey the voice of the LORD our God."
>
> Jeremiah 42:6

A man who has friends must himself be friendly, but there is a friend who sticks closer than a brother.

Proverbs 18:24

"I am so lonely. I mean . . . I have friends, but I feel totally alone." We all get lonely at times. The freaky thing is that you could be in the middle of a thousand people and still feel alone. When the feelings of loneliness consume us, our gut reaction is to totally shut out other people. But avoiding people just feeds the loneliness. Fight the urge to push people out. Open up. Talk with a friend. Let them know that you're feeling lonely and you just need to hang out.

EXTREME FOR JESUS

> "When you do a charitable deed, do not let your left hand know what your right hand is doing."
> **Matthew 6:3**

Show me the money! Somewhere we have gone spastic with our idea of money. Sure, money is needed. And most of us have what we need. But there are lots of people who don't. They have some major needs. Here's an extreme challenge: Get some friends together and look around your neighborhood, your church, your street. Find a need. Then, figure out how to fill it—whatever it takes. Money, time, wood, paint . . . whatever it takes. Find the need and fill it—but don't brag about it afterwards. You'll start with an "I am giving to you" attitude. But by the time you finish, you'll get a lot more than you gave.

> If anyone thinks himself to be
> something, when he is nothing,
> he deceives himself.

Galatians 6:3

It's very easy to be something to your friends you're actually not. As a matter of fact, you may find that your personality changes depending on which group of people you're hanging out with. When you're with your smart friends you act smart. When with your athletic friends you act like an athlete. You've done this so often and for so long, you've almost forgotten who you really are. It's an easy trap to get into and hard to get out of. Ask God to get you out of the trap and see the person you really are. You'll probably discover how much you like the person you really are and enjoy not having to act so much. Get real.

"It's your lucky day."
"You lucky bum!"
"Thank my lucky stars."
Ever used any of those
sayings? Ever feel like you
don't have any luck? Well,
you're right. You don't.
Luck is not for Christians.
You might be flipping a
coin for something, but

> The lot is cast into the lap, but its every decision is from the LORD.
>
> **Proverbs 16:33**

how it lands is all under God's control. When
you see someone who seems to have all the
luck, they don't. And when you think you have
none, you don't. What seems like bad luck to
you might be a blessing in disguise. Like when
Joseph was sold into slavery. What could have
been called really bad luck turned out to be a
true blessing for the whole country. What's going on in your life that looks like bad luck?
How could God use it for good?

He gives power to the weak, and to those who have no might He increases strength.

Isaiah 40:29

You are in a room, a dark room. All around you the enemy advances. They're coming at you with swords and knives to torture and kill you. On the floor is a sword. A shiny, heavy, powerful sword. Do you pick it up and fight, or do you just look at it? The Word of God is *your* sword. It is useful for battle—the battle of the mind— even when you feel like giving up. You feel too weak to press on, too defeated to ever win again, then you must at all costs pick up the sword. With each swing of the mighty blade the enemy is silenced. God promises that He will renew your strength and give you power to be all that you should be.

EXTREME FOR JESUS

"Most assuredly, I say to you, whatever you ask the Father in My name He will give you."

John 16:23

Praying in Jesus' name is more than just a series of words that we might piece together to get God to make our wishes come true. God wants us to see His Son as the only way that we can approach Him. When we pray in Jesus' name, we're telling God that we believe what Jesus said is true, and that we know He agrees with our requests. Think about how easy it is to talk to an adult when you're friends with their son or daughter. Is your relationship with Jesus so close that His Father knows who you are?

> Rejoice always, pray without ceasing, in everything give thanks; for this is the will of God in Christ Jesus for you.
>
> **1 Thessalonians 5:16-18**

My summer missions partner and I were surprised when our supervisor told us that our new clothes had been stolen out of our truck. In spite of our shock, we began to thank the Lord that the thief had at least left our food! We had no control over any of the circumstances, but because of what God's Word says, we knew what our reaction had to be—to praise God in the middle of the trouble. That day we also began praying that the thief would return our stuff. We continued at it day after day. About three weeks later, sure enough, we got a telephone call from the police telling us that our clothes had been found. Will you look past your circumstances today and rejoice in the Lord? Will you praise Him just for who He is?

Hurry up and wait. That's what we spend a lot of time doing. Waiting. It seems like we have to wait for all kinds of things. Wait to download, wait in line, wait for our little brother to get out of the bathroom. But sometimes God tells us to wait. It is like we're praying and wanting something to happen now, but God is taking His own sweet time. If you've been really praying about something and haven't heard anything from God, try—it will be hard, but try—to just chill and wait. Look and see if you can tell what He is doing around you.

> Wait on the LORD; be of good courage, and He shall strengthen your heart; wait, I say, on the LORD!
>
> Psalm 27:14

> Stand fast therefore in the liberty by which Christ has made us free, and do not be entangled again with a yoke of bondage.
>
> Galatians 5:1

Handcuffs. Ever been in them? It's not a fun party. It doesn't seem like they're that big of a deal. But when they're slapped around your wrist and tightened down, they become a big deal. You can't move your arms, and when you try to, they just get tighter. That's the way Satan works. He wants to get us locked up by making bad decisions. Then once he has us, he wants us to try to fight to get out of the mess on our own. The more we try, the tighter his grip gets. Listen, God holds the key to get out of the sin that keeps you a prisoner. Ask Him to unlock the handcuffs. Then stop putting them back on yourself.

EXTREME FOR JESUS

He rejected the advice which the elders had given him, and consulted the young men who had grown up with him.

1 Kings 12:8

There it is. The best mountain bike available on the market, and you want it. You would do anything to get it. The problem is that you don't really have the money for it. The only real option is to use the money you've been saving for college. What to do? You ask your parents; they don't like the idea much and advise you against buying it. Your friends think now is the time and convince you to buy the bike anyway. Six months later you're out of school, wanting to go to college, but you have no money. You wrecked the bike, and it is now worth only a small fraction of its original value. Guess what? You should've taken your parents' advice.

Do all things without complaining and disputing.

Philippians 2:14

Here is your challenge for today: Don't complain—not about anything. I'm not kidding. Just try it for one day. It's not that easy. But it *is* commanded. How do we find so much to complain about? "It's too hot. It's too cold. I hate this food. She's so mean." Imagine a friend who complains about everything you do for her. The meal was too cold, the gift too small, the hug too tight. How unappreciated would you feel? Remember that God has put you exactly where you are to experience just what you need to experience. He gives the rain to nourish the plants; the heat to warm the earth; the mean person to teach you grace. So don't complain; instead, thank Him. I promise you, you'll see a change in your life that only a positive attitude can bring.

We Christians have a certain hope that nonbelievers don't have. We have a confidence in life—being certain of our salvation (Romans 10:9); certain that God works all things for our good (Romans 8:28); and certain of our inheritance (Ephesians 1:14). When someone asks you why you believe all that stuff about Jesus, do you have an answer for them? Paul says we

> Always be ready to give a defense to everyone who asks you a reason for the hope that is in you.
>
> **1 Peter 3:15**

should "always" be ready to give a reason why we believe. That doesn't mean we fight over it, but we need to know why we believe. If you don't know why you believe in Jesus, then find out. Read the Word. Learn His truths. Keep Scripture in your heart so you can answer the question, "Why do you believe all that?"

"From the rising of the sun, even to its going down, My name shall be great among the Gentiles; in every place incense shall be offered to My name, and a pure offering; for My name shall be great among the nations," says the LORD of hosts.

Malachi 1:11

Every few years a really talented athlete will come along and break all the records. For awhile they're everybody's hero . . . until the next great athlete comes along and beats their record. Being great only lasts until someone younger and more talented comes along. The good news is, the rules aren't the same in the spirit world. God's record can't be broken. He will always be the ultimate, no matter what changes our culture goes through. People everywhere, throughout all time, will always know that God rules. Do your actions show God's reputation?

EXTREME FOR JESUS

If the foot should say, "Because I am not a hand, I am not of the body," is it therefore not of the body?

1 Corinthians 12:15

"**I** hate math. I don't like it. I don't get it. I am so stupid." Sound familiar? Listen, math may not be your thing. But don't beat yourself up. Maybe you're better at acting, or baseball, or building things. Maybe you're a good listener or a good singer. We all have been given different gifts and talents to use. What is it that you like to do and are good at? Talk to your parents, guidance counselor at school, or others who have the same strengths and abilities as you do. Find ways to use your gifts, then you'll be fulfilling God's design for you.

A perverse man sows strife,
and a whisperer separates the
best of friends.

Proverbs 16:28

"Did you hear about Rachel? I heard that this weekend she went down to the . . . ." Wait a minute. What's going on here? There's nothing intelligent to talk about, so you just talk about other people? Rumors. Gossip. You know what? Gossip is like a dog that doesn't bark. He sits there, wags his tail, then when you least expect it . . . CHOMP! Gossip seems harmless at first—especially when you're the one spreading it. But watch out. As soon as you turn your back . . . CHOMP! You'll be attacked by gossip yourself. So take a stand. Don't be a part of destroying someone else by spreading rumors.

Thursday

Thank God it doesn't say, "Do not be angry." Anger is a natural emotion that we're allowed to feel, but must control. If you're angry with someone, don't just brood over it. You have to do something about it. Staying mad only gives Satan a foothold, which can lead to a stranglehold. God forgave you; you can forgive others. Determine your motives. Why are you angry? What in *you*—not in the other person—causes it? How can you learn more about yourself? Jesus had a lot to be angry about. But as He hung on the cross while the crowd mocked Him, He asked God to forgive them. He did not allow Himself to be consumed with anger. You can make that same choice.

"Be angry, and do not sin": do not let the sun go down on your wrath.

Ephesians 4:26

> In all these things we are more than conquerors through Him who loved us.
>
> Romans 8:37

Have you ever lost anything? The big game, your best friend, your reputation? Have you ever been broken, beaten down? Have you just lost too much? Your parents are gone, your virginity is gone? Is there any hope? The answer is yes. So pick yourself up and dust yourself off, because you are more than a conqueror. The battle rages. The chariots race, the blood spews, the horses fall, and there you are in the middle of it. This life is a battle, but you are more than a conqueror—even if you don't feel like it. God promises you that nothing can separate you from His love. Not an air raid, not an enemy invasion, not a full-scale attack. Stand on His promise and feel the blood of a conqueror surge through your veins.

Whoever guards his mouth
and tongue keeps his soul
from troubles.

Proverbs 21:23

Has your tongue ever gotten you into
trouble? Ever boasted or bragged
about something you can do? You may not
be someone who goes around with a big
mouth or anything. But how well do you
control your tongue in other situations?
Ever hurt a friend by a smart comeback?
Can you keep a secret? Do you always tell
the truth, even if it will make your life a
trauma? Do you speak in ways to build
other people up instead of tearing them
down? Stay out of trouble by guarding what
you say; ask God to give you love in how
you use your tongue today.

Flee also youthful lusts; but pursue righteousness.

2 Timothy 2:22

The story is told of a man who wished to hire a stagecoach driver to take him across a mountainous pass. The first man interviewed bragged that he could drive keeping his wheels only an inch from the edge. The second man boasted that he could keep half of the wheels hanging over the edge. Finally, an older, wiser man was interviewed and said, "I don't know how close I can get to the edge. I stay as far away from it as possible." He was the one hired. Too many times we're like the first two men in the story. We ask questions like, "How far is too far?" when it comes to the physical part of a relationship. We should be more like the older, wiser man and try to stay as far away from the edge as possible—just to be sure we don't fall off the edge.

E-mail has changed our lives. More people are writing one another than ever before, and in most cases the message can get there in just a matter of seconds. There's something so cool about checking your e-mail and having a message from a friend pop up in your inbox. Getting e-mail somehow just makes our day!

> I thank my God upon every remembrance of you.
>
> Philippians 1:3

When Paul wrote a letter to friends, he encouraged them right from the start. Is there someone you need to encourage today? Who needs to hear your voice or get your e-mail? Just a simple "hello" or "I was thinking about you" can make a huge difference in someone's life!

Where there is no counsel, the people fall; but in the multitude of counselors there is safety.

Proverbs 11:14

Oh, yeah. Here we go! It's hot enough to use the cement as a frying pan. The only word you got to say is . . . cannonball! You run to the edge of the pool and take a flying leap with your body tucked in a tight ball. Right when you brace for the big splash you see the sign: "Warning: Pool drained for repairs." Talk about pain!

There are things that happen sometimes that could've been avoided if we'd just read the warning signs. God loves you. He doesn't want to see you hurt. He loves you so much He made sure there are warning signs everywhere. Read His Word. Seek counsel from godly friends. Pay attention to the warning signs.

EXTREME FOR JESUS

"He is like a man building a house, who dug deep and laid the foundation on the rock."
Luke 6:48

Jody jumps his motorcycle 90 feet into the air. His feet fly. He looks like Superman hanging in the air. When you think there is no time left, he pulls himself back on and lands perfectly. It's called freestyling. The pros say the most important parts of freestyling are the takeoff and the landing. Who cares what tricks you can do if you can't land. The awesome tricks are built on a solid, basic foundation.

Your life is the same. Your successes, your happiness, in life have to start with a solid foundation—knowing Christ as Lord. The foundation is made stronger through prayer, reading the Bible, and going to church. That gets you the winning jump in life.

> The horse is prepared for the day of battle, but deliverance is of the LORD.

Proverbs 21:31

Some days it might seem like you're on the front lines. The enemy is attacking from all sides. You hide in your foxhole; bullets are flying. "Why me?" you moan. I'll tell you why. If you were in a war and you had to send your troops to attack the enemy, would you attack the troops who are doing nothing, or would you attack the ones on the front lines? Satan causes you grief because you're important to God. If you weren't, then he wouldn't bother. A child of God is his archenemy. And the more extreme for Jesus you are, the more he'll see you as a threat. But take heart—this is part of the adventure of life. And God promises that the victory is His.

What's the difference between punishment and discipline? "Punishment" is *to inflict a penalty*. "Discipline" is *training of the mind or body or moral faculties; subjection to authority, self-control*. Punishment has to do with getting what you deserve for doing something bad. Discipline can be for bad stuff, but it is meant to

> He who disdains instruction [discipline] despises his own soul, but he who heeds rebuke gets understanding.
>
> **Proverbs 15:32**

teach you to avoid the bad stuff in the future. It is also used as training and instruction. You can discipline yourself to work out every day. You can discipline yourself to pray. So discipline isn't necessarily a bad thing. In fact, it's an opportunity to gain understanding and growth. When you're being disciplined, look at it as an opportunity to grow in wisdom and understanding. You'll lose in the end if you ignore discipline. So be thankful that you're being taught now so that you'll benefit later.

Do you not know that we shall judge angels? How much more, things that pertain to this life?

1 Corinthians
6:3

Angels seem to be all the rage these days. People are writing books and making movies all about them. Hollywood wants us to think that when someone dies, they suddenly sprout wings and become an angel. Angels are a reminder of the intriguing unseen world, but they're not dead people that have come back to life. The Word doesn't say that angels have been created in the image of God like we have. And they're not a way to get to God. But they do set an example for us in obedience and worship. Don't ever put the creation above the Creator. Study all of God's creation to see how amazing He is.

EXTREME FOR JESUS

> If we confess our sins, He is faithful and just to forgive us our sins.
> **1 John 1:9**

Repeat these words: "If it's forgiven, it's forgotten." There are no "sin scales" in heaven that measure how bad you've been and put you beyond the reach of God's love. He wants you to be close to Him. He has already given His life for you, so forgiveness is no farther than a prayer away. All the shame and guilt that goes along with sin cannot compare to the totally awesome, outta-this-world feeling of being forgiven. And God says, "All you have to do is ask." You don't want to live with the load of sin on your back, do you? Let God take it and throw it away, never to be seen or remembered again . . . ever. God will not remind you of the things you've done. They're forgiven and, for as long as eternity, they're forgotten.

> Do you not know that your body is the temple of the Holy Spirit ... and you are not your own?

1 Corinthians 6:19

Hey couch potatoes! How's that temple of yours doing? Yeah, that's right. Your body is the *temple* of God. Would you go to your own house and torch the furniture. That's exactly what is happening to God's temple when you light a cigarette to smoke. Would you go home and rip out all of the electricity and think, "No one will ever know"? That's what's happening when you use alcohol or drugs. You're destroying the electrical wiring in your mind. Listen, you only have one body. Take care of it. Stay away from things you know will destroy it. And hey, get off the Internet. Peel yourself away from the video games. And take your "temple" for a walk.

Thursday

Music can be very healing. There's a reason why we use music for worship. It connects us to God faster than anything. David got this. As he was on the run from Saul, he wrote many songs of pain. He found relief in music. If you have deep feelings you can't seem to express to God, pick up the Book of Psalms and read to Him. Or find a great song that expresses your feelings and sing it to God. You're not alone. Many songwriters feel just like you. Use music in your worship. Use it in your quiet time. And be healed through the music.

> How long shall I take counsel in my soul, having sorrow in my heart daily?
>
> **Psalm 13:2**

If there is anything praiseworthy—meditate on these things . . . and the God of peace will be with you.

Philippians 4:8-9

Our thoughts control our feelings. However we think is how we will feel. Would you like to feel peace and joy? Paul gives us the recipe. Rather than fill your mind with all the terrible things in this world, choose—and I say choose because it really is a choice—to think about the things that are great, holy, or just plain cool. When you focus on the good rather than the bad, your feelings will go from bad to good. Your loneliness will split because you'll notice God is there. Your resentment will walk away as you thank God for your life. Write down six things you're thankful for. This will get your positive juices flowing and put you in line with what God wants for you.

EXTREME FOR JESUS

> For they loved the praise of men more than the praise of God.
> **John 12:43**

The crowd goes wild as you sink the final game-winning shot. All the team lifts you up on their shoulders and parades you around the court. You're the star. You saved the game. If it weren't for you, your team would be in the locker room getting chewed out by the coach. How does it feel to be praised?

New scene: The crowd around you is screaming, "Drink!" They are challenging you to be cool and part of the crowd. Can you resist the temptation to please them? Can you walk away from the potential "points" you could score with this group? God whispers in your ear, "Walk away; say no." You hear Him, but He's so quiet and their cheers are so loud. Who will you choose? Who will you impress? It's your choice.

> When desire has conceived, it
> gives birth to sin; and sin,
> when it is full-grown, brings
> forth death.
>
> James 1:15

Brent and Julia are one "hot" couple. Popularity, good looks, and a stand for Christ all make the package nice and sparkly. They talked often about how wonderful it would be to "do it" whenever they liked. One night they went all the way, and it soon became a regular occurrence. They were only seventeen. Both of them had dreams. Julia wanted to go to the mission field, and Brent was a football star until . . . well you know the rest.

Be careful what you think. It will become what you say. Be careful what you say. It will become what you do. Be careful what you do. It will become a habit.

Tuesday

Picture this: You have just won an award for being the most humble person in the world. The only bummer is that when people heard you pre-pared an acceptance speech, they took it away from you because they thought you were being too proud. What in the world is the point in being humble? The really cool thing about humility is that it doesn't ask for rewards for doing good things. No reward, you say? That's right; no reward. No nothin'. When we have the opportunity to serve, we need to do it without expecting to be noticed or even thanked. God will give us the reward we deserve in His time. For now be rewarded by the fact that we're totally blessing someone for no reason at all. Greatness is serving. Strive to be legendary.

> Humble your-selves in the sight of the Lord, and He will lift you up.
>
> James 4:10

By whom a person is overcome, by him also he is brought into bondage.

2 Peter 2:19

Sure, you've been smoking for awhile, but you claim you're not addicted. It's only a couple of cigarettes a day. Really no big deal, and you can stop anytime. Or maybe it's your boyfriend or girlfriend that's overbearing, and you do everything they say. You say you're not that committed and could break up at any time, but you never do. Maybe it's time to come to grips with the fact that you've been mastered by something without even knowing it. (Or maybe you know it, but just don't want to admit it.) You think that you're in control, but nothing in your life shows that. Turn your course and let God be your master.

EXTREME FOR JESUS

> "He who is least among you all will be great."
>
> **Luke 9:48**

"If you don't play to win, don't play." "Second place is the first-place loser." Everything the world offers tells us that we have to be number one. We have to have the best. Companies spend billions of dollars a year to convince us that their product is the best and, if we buy it, then we will be number one. That is a straight-out lie. Check out the truth. The Bible says that if you want to be number one, you have to step aside and help others get ahead. If you really want to live the way Jesus lived, then look around. See who needs help. Don't worry about yourself. Figure out how to help others who seem to be struggling. Do that and you'll find the answer to the question, "What would Jesus do?"

> He said, "I heard Your voice in the garden, and I was afraid because I was naked; and I hid myself."

Genesis 3:10

Hiding from God. What was Adam thinking? God—omniscient, omnipresent—wouldn't find him behind a tree? What a silly idea, Adam, you goof! Of course God knew where you were. He even knew why you were hiding.

Have *you* ever tried to hide from God? You avoid talking to Him or avoid church so that you won't be found out? You goof! There is nowhere to hide. David was "a man after God's own heart," because he didn't hide from God. If you're tempted to hide from God, stop kidding yourself and come out into the open. The longer you hide, the worse it gets. Let God know you've sinned. It's called confession, and it truly is good for the soul.

Did you know that there's power in your words? That's right, power. With a word you can destroy someone or build up someone. Do you know how it feels when

> Comfort each other and edify one another.
>
> 1 Thessalonians 5:11

people encourage you? When they tell you how good you are or how smart you are? Suddenly there's a little more fuel in your tank. Your engines start to rev, and you begin to think you can do just about anything. Well, you can do that for others, too. Leaders have found that people will rise or fall to meet others' expectations of them. If you encourage people with your words, you can bring success into their lives. A lot of your friends probably don't get much encouragement at home. Find some ways today that you can build up people. Give them wings to soar, and they'll be your friends forever.

Where can I go from Your Spirit? Or where can I flee from Your presence?

Psalm 139:7

How would you conduct yourself if you knew that someone you totally looked up to was watching you? Would you be doing the same things on Friday and Saturday nights? Would you tell the same jokes? OK, you know the next question. What if Jesus was standing next to you? What then? Same movie? Same joke? He's always with us you know. And He *does* see everything that we do and hear all that we say. That should be a comforting thought. But it can also be very uncomfortable if we are inconsistent in our behavior. What actions or attitudes in your life is Jesus not too hyped about?

When He had made a whip of cords, He drove them all out of the temple . . . and poured out the changers' money and overturned the tables.

John 2:15

EXTREME FOR JESUS

Jesus was angry that people had turned the temple into a flea market—hocking their wares right and left in some kind of money-hungry frenzy. God desires that we keep the temple uncluttered, giving props to things that are holy, and staying away from the things of this world that mess us up. Jesus knew that those people were in it just to make money, and it ticked Him off. Are there things that have come into your life that may be turning your temple into a flea market? You better clear it out before He does, and save yourself a little grief.

> Rejoice in the Lord always.
> Again I will say, rejoice!
>
> Philippians 4:4

You just got your report card and it's all A's. Your grandma just sent you a hundred dollars as an "I love you" gift. Mom and Dad gave you your own set of keys to the car and agreed to let you go to Hawaii with your friends as a graduation present. Everything in your life is going great . . . no, excellent. So what's wrong. You seem a little depressed or upset. It's because the boy who broke up with you a month ago is sitting three rows away in your algebra class. It's a common issue. We have a lot that goes well in our life, but we can't take our eyes off of the one little negative. Learn to focus on the positive. If you don't see any positive, remember that you're a child of God. That should carry a lot of weight.

I dare you! You say you're a Christian. I dare you to prove it. You say you're extreme for Jesus. I dare you to take a stand. I dare you to take up for a dorky kid who is getting picked on. I dare you to tell a friend about your salvation through Jesus. I dare you to stand up to the world and its temptations. I dare you to be loud. To say no to partying, sex, lying. I dare you to live out what you say you believe. You say you're extreme for Jesus. Prove it. I dare you.

> "If anyone desires to come after Me, let him deny himself, and take up his cross, and follow Me."
>
> Matthew 16:24

Deliver those who are drawn toward death, and hold back those stumbling to the slaughter. If you say, "Surely we did not know this," does not He who weighs the hearts consider it?

Proverbs
24:11-12

Imagine it: hundreds of people staggering in a daze, zombielike as they line up to be the next to be slaughtered, exterminated. We've seen it in history; we've seen it in the news—"ethnic cleansing" they call it. What if you could come in and rescue them all from certain death? Would you do it or just mourn their suffering? We have life to offer those around us. We can bring them out of their bondage and into freedom. Next time you can share Jesus with someone, don't be afraid that they won't want Him. Remember, they're stumbling toward slaughter, and we can save them. So be bold and compassionate as you give them hope.

Do not forget my law, but let your heart keep my commands.

Proverbs 3:1

What do you know by heart? Your favorite song? The game plays? Trivia? Probably a lot of things. Things you need to know, like phone numbers, and things you don't need to know, like lines from movies. Some things you know might save a life, like 911 or CPR. And other things can give you peace and long life. If you knew you could get that by memorizing something, would it be worth it to you? The Bible promises that if you carry the Word of God in your heart—like you do the phone number of your best friend—you'll have peace and joy and much more. God didn't give us His Word for the occasional read; He gave it to us to live by. So choose a verse that means a lot to you and memorize it today.

> ## Whatever you do in word or deed, do all in the name of the Lord Jesus.
>
> ### Colossians 3:17

I remember hearing the story of a young man who cleaned tables at a local restaurant. He told a friend of mine that, as he wiped down each table, he would pray and ask blessing on the people who had just finished eating and on those who would be sitting there next. Can you imagine the impact that the Lord has in that place as this one employee chooses to clean tables to the glory of God, while blessing others in the process? I'm encouraged by the fact that this is an ordinary man who does incredible things through His obedience to God. Make a list of some of the things you're involved in today. Choose to complete them for the Lord. He is your Boss.

The race is on. Your opponent is climbing the wall as fast as you are. It's an extreme obstacle course. The adrenaline rush is pushing you over the edge. It's a killer, but it's worth it. We all have obstacles in our lives. We each have things we have to overcome. Drug addiction, alcoholism, abortion, abuse . . . whatever. You can either move on, or stay. You can't do both. If you have something you can't get past, go talk to someone—your youth pastor, counselor, mom, teacher, someone you can count on. They will help you get over the obstacle so you can run through life on the edge.

> "My grace is sufficient for you, for My strength is made perfect in weakness."
>
> 2 Corinthians 12:9

> "The eyes of the LORD run to and fro throughout the whole earth, to show Himself strong on behalf of those whose heart is loyal to Him."
>
> 2 Chronicles 16:9

When you climb to the top of a mountain, what do you see? Your view seems to be at least a thousand miles or more. What areas of interest stick out to you? A lake? Another mountain in the distance? The small town several miles away? It's all beautiful and breathtaking, yet certain things stand out. You know what God is looking for when He looks at us? He specifically looks for those people who are faithful and loyal to Him. Does He see you there?

EXTREME FOR JESUS

"There is no one who has left house or parents or brothers or wife or children, for the sake of the kingdom of God, who shall not receive many times more in this present time, and in the age to come eternal life."
Luke 18:29-30

What are you staking your life on? What are you relying on to rock your world? Does God want you to give that up? Why? Maybe *He* wants to rock your world. If you're relying on something else, where is God? What are you putting your money on? Your favorite video game, the Net, shopping? Maybe even friends? Here's how to figure it out. What's the first thing you put on your schedule every day? Jesus asked people to give up everything they owned in order to follow Him more radically. What could you let go of to let God totally rock your world?

> Now the Lord is the Spirit; and where the Spirit of the Lord is, there is liberty.

2 Corinthians 3:17

Liberty is freedom from bondage. Isn't it funny that most nonbelievers think that they have more freedom than we do? They see our list of rules and laws as bondage. But what they don't know is that the boundaries God has given us are what *give* us freedom. Who is in more bondage: someone who has to drink to feel happy, or someone who is high on God? Don't believe that a Christian has less freedom, because the law *is* freedom. If you're obedient to God, you won't be a slave to alcohol or drugs, to fashion, or to cliques. You won't be a slave to gambling or being thin. You'll be free to be who God made you—a work of art.

A lot of people think this means you should tell everybody exactly what you think. Tell them the truth even if it hurts. If she's ugly, then

> Do not lie to one another.
> Colossians 3:9

tell her. If you think his painting is awful, tell him. If he really bugs you when he chomps his food, tell him. But this verse does not give permission to hurt one another. Remember that if what you have to say is not useful for building a person up, then you don't need to say it. So don't abuse this scripture and claim it as you hurl insults at people. Instead, check your heart and measure your motives. See if it will make their life better if you tell them, and if it's something they really need to know. Measure your words carefully. Chances are, you won't get in trouble for being slow to speak.

No man can tame the tongue. It is an unruly evil, full of deadly poison.

James 3:8

"I was just playing with you!" is what we usually say when we've said something that has hurt someone's feelings. Every now and then we take our "joking around" a little too far. Then we find out really quick that what we thought was funny has turned into something destructive.

The Bible says our tongue is like a deadly poison. That means it has the power to destroy or even kill. Wow! We must realize that we have a big responsibility to choose our words carefully. Our friends, family, teachers, and others cannot be protected from the power of our words. Make it your prayer that God will give you the strength to say the right things to others.

EXTREME FOR JESUS

> "And then I will declare to them, 'I never knew you; depart from Me.'"
>
> **Matthew 7:23**

"Is that your final answer?" We all know where we've heard that before, right? Well, here's a question for you. Who wants to be a sold-out Christian? Jesus is your lifeline and your friends are there to help. The rest is up to you. After this life is over, we will have to face up to the way we served God. Have you ever thought about what God will say to you when you see Him? What will you say to Him? "I got by all right, didn't I?" or "God, I've done all I could to serve You with all I had." Be ready to live for God the way Jesus died for you—all out and unashamed. Are you a fervent servant or a sublime pantomime? Is that your final answer?

> Godly sorrow produces repentance leading to salvation, not to be regretted; but the sorrow of the world produces death.
>
> 2 Corinthians 7:10

What do you regret? Missing your prom? Last weekend? Yelling at your mom? Going too far? Failing a test? There are things that we do that will make us look back and say, "Man, I am so stupid." God knows that we have regrets about some things we do. But it doesn't have to be that way. If we recognize that what we did was wrong, stop doing it, and follow God, then we'll learn from our mistakes and we'll be stronger. If we grow stronger in our faith, we'll truly live with no regrets! What is something that you regret? Tell God about it. Ask Him to help you move past the regret.

Character is doing the right thing because it's the right thing—not because it's cool, or popular, but simply because it's the *right* thing. It's easy for us to think that we're going to change other people by hanging out with them. We know that a group of our friends doesn't have the best reputation. But we're strong. We can change them. The person we're dating is not a Christian, but we're OK with that because we will change them. Wake up! Read the scripture again. Does it say that good company will change bad company? No. So be careful. Surround yourself with other Christians. Invite them to hang out with you. Strengthen each other so you'll be able to maintain good character while you're in bad company.

> Do not be deceived: "Evil company corrupts good habits."
>
> 1 Corinthians 15:33

> Without counsel, plans go awry, but in the multitude of counselors they are established.
>
> **Proverbs 15:22**

Are you trying to figure out God's will? There is a way to find out. Three things should line up in order to know if something is God's will. First is God's Word. What you're considering must not be against His Word. Second is the Holy Spirit. The Holy Spirit will make it clear in prayer. And third is godly advice. If you think that you're too wise to need advice, then you're a fool. If you don't have a few godly advisors in your life, find some. Choose people who'll tell you what God wants you to hear, not what you want to hear. This will save you a lot of heartache in the end. So seek godly counselors. You might not need them now, but one day soon you will.

EXTREME FOR JESUS

Do not be drunk with wine, in which is dissipation; but be filled with the Spirit.

Ephesians 5:18

People get drunk to fill a need. They have a need to get away, to change their life, their personality, their outlook on life. They're empty and they hope that booze will fill them up. But you, as a Christian, are filled with the Holy Spirit. That empty place in you was filled when you asked Jesus into your heart. He's your pain reliever. Drinking to relieve the pain is like putting a piece of masking tape over your check-engine light in the car. It covers up the evidence of the problem, but does nothing *about* the problem itself. If you feel you need an escape, ask God what the real problem is. Until you solve that, you'll always be running on empty, seeking whatever you can to cover up the pain.

> Do not think it strange concerning the fiery trial which is to try you, as though some strange thing happened to you; but rejoice to the extent that you partake of Christ's sufferings.
>
> 1 Peter 4:12-13

Did you know that the hatching process almost kills a chicken? Those cute little chicks aren't very strong, and it's tough to get out of the shell. By the time it's hatched, the chick is almost dead. But don't help! If someone were to come by and crack the egg to help him out, the chick would die for sure. Hatching from the egg gives him enough strength to survive life. Maybe that's why we hurt so much. Is God unfair because He lets us struggle sometimes? Or does He let us learn, and love us enough to let us be strengthened through our struggles? How have your struggles made you stronger?

Tuesday

Did you know that rat poison is 99.9% good ingredients? The rats are attracted to it and eat it because it tastes good to them. It's only the extremely small amount of poison that kills the rat. This is a trick that Satan has perfected. He's taken lots of things in our lives that, in and of themselves, can be good things—things like music, movies, etc. But he's mixed them with poison. Many times we try to justify what we listen to or watch by saying, "I don't listen to the words" or "It has a really good plot." But poison is poison, and even a little can hurt you spiritually.

> Do you not know that a little leaven leavens the whole lump?
>
> **1 Corinthians 5:6**

"Most assuredly, I say to you, he who hears My word and believes in Him who sent Me has everlasting life, and shall not come into judgment, but has passed from death into life."

John 5:24

All you have to do is believe and make Him Lord? Could it be that easy? Is it the real deal? It's kind of like a fancy restaurant advertising a free dinner. Some would be all over it and chow down. But most people would stay away, thinking there must be some kind of catch involved. God's totally free gift of eternal life is as easy as that free meal. No strings, no lines, no kidding, no charge. Eternal life—free for the taking.

EXTREME FOR JESUS

> Whatever a man sows, that he will also reap.
> **Galatians 6:7**

There once was a farmer who planted tomato seeds. He worked all day, dug the earth, buried the seeds, and watered what he hoped would be a fantastic crop of corn. What? Corn? But he planted tomato seeds. What was he thinking? When you plant tomatoes, you get . . . drum roll, please . . . *tomatoes!* Duh!

Have you ever thought about the end of your life? What people will say at your funeral? Who will come? What you will leave behind? What you do today will answer those questions for you. If you plant the seed of negativity, you will lead a depressed life. If you plant the seed of generosity, you will experience contentment. Think today what you want to be remembered for. Begin now to sow those seeds so that someday you can reap the harvest of your dreams.

> You have become estranged
> from Christ, you who attempt
> to be justified by law; you
> have fallen from grace.

Galatians 5:4

Have you ever broken the rules and been thrown off the team? Lied to a friend and lost the friendship? Have you ever been punished for doing what you weren't supposed to do? In life, to avoid punishment we follow the rules. It's the same with God. Maybe you think, "If I break a rule, I'm out. He won't love me as much. I'll be dropped from the team." Do you follow the rules just to please God? Paul tells us that's backwards. Our sin was paid for the day He hung on the cross. Follow the rules because you love God, not because you want to save your hide. Are you following the law in order to get something from God or out of pure love for Him?

What do you want to do with your life? Not what your parents want you to do or your friends or your teachers, but you. What do you really want to accomplish? What is the desire that is deep inside of you? Guess what? God knows that desire. In fact, He gave you all the godly desires in your heart. He places within you a desire that won't die. Your job is to grow that God-given desire. What would it take to make this desire a reality? Write down how you can accomplish it. Every day do one thing that will bring you one step closer to your God-given dreams.

> Delight yourself also in the LORD, and He shall give you the desires of your heart.
>
> **Psalm 37:4**

For this reason I also suffer these things; nevertheless I am not ashamed, for I know whom I have believed and am persuaded that He is able to keep what I have committed to Him until that Day.

2 Timothy 1:12

Do you set exceptions for people? Have you ever been disappointed? Join the crowd. People will always let us down. There's no way out of that. Getting a grip on the fact that God isn't like the rest is hard. When we feel let down by God, it's really more a problem of the way we're looking at it than it is of God's behavior. Turn your expectations around. Expect God to *know* what is best. Look at the lives of people who have trusted in Him. Then list some of the ways God has totally bailed them. Learn from them and trust Him with your life.

EXTREME FOR JESUS

Jesus wept.
John 11:35

One of my friends lost his mother in a car accident, and it swept him off his feet. He was crushed and devastated. His Christian friends were there and helped him through the toughest time of his life. He had always been the type of guy who was too tough to cry or even to smile in pictures. Now he's different. He's a new man. He figured out that it's all right for him to cry. It doesn't mean that he's not tough; it just means he's human.

Jesus cried when He found out that Lazarus had died. He showed us that it's OK to cry and have emotions. Christ loves us just as He loved Lazarus. Thank God today for showing us how to love deeply and how to express our emotions.

Love . . . is not provoked.

1 Corinthians 13:4-5

Some people go through life like Joe Cool; nothing bothers them. Others are more like Homer Simpson; they blow their top all the time over the least little thing. Most of us are somewhere in between. Listen, God isn't saying you can't ever be angry. What He is saying is this: It should take a lot to make you angry. Why? Because love is about forgiveness. This makes sense since God is love, and God has forgiven you. Practice patience with others. Let God's love control your anger.

Do you know Michael Jordan? Yes? Do you know him, or do you know *about* him? Have you ever sat down and talked with him? Yeah, right! There's a difference between knowing some- one and knowing about someone. Lots of people know *about* Jesus. They even know He's the Son of God. But they've never made Him Lord. They know all the right things to say, but they don't know Him. Even the demons of hell know *about* Jesus. How about you? Have you told God that you know you're a sinner and you need Him to forgive you? Asked Him to take control of your life? If you've already done that, do something today that will help you get to know Him better.

> That I may know Him and the power of His resurrection.
>
> **Philippians 3:10**

Without shedding of blood there is no remission.

Hebrews 9:22

Do you know why the *Titanic* was such a disaster? It was because there were not enough lifeboats onboard. That meant that either a few could live or they all would die. If everyone would've insisted on getting in the lifeboats, then the boats would have sunk from the load, and no one would have survived. So, many gave their lives so that others could live. Would you be able to choose death so someone else could be saved?

Jesus chose death so that you could be saved. He shed His blood on the cross so that anyone and everyone could be released from the guilt and penalty of their sins. All we have to do is ask.

EXTREME FOR JESUS

A friend loves at all times,
and a brother is born
for adversity.
Proverbs 17:17

A friend loves at all times. What if they're totally cruel to me? A friend loves at all times. What if they dis me in front of everybody? A friend loves at all times. What if they hurt my feelings? A friend loves at all times. What if they walk away from our friendship? A friend loves at all times. ARGH! This friendship thing is hard. Especially when you're the only one "loving at all times." But just like all the other commands in Scripture, this one has its rewards. How can you love at all times? When can you turn the other cheek? Has someone offended you? Will you love them? Has someone cheated you? Will you love them? Will you love them at all times?

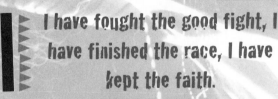

> I have fought the good fight, I have finished the race, I have kept the faith.
>
> 2 Timothy 4:7

Remember running baton races in school? Someone on your team would make their trek around the course and then hand off the baton to you? You had to wait for them to make those final yards before it was your turn to run with it. Then, with all of your strength and endurance you ran *your* part of the race.

God's Word has been given to us. We have been entered into the race of life. It's up to us to use all of our strength and endurance to complete what God has called us to do. Be set on fire by God's Word. Read it. Know it. Then set your eyes on the finish line of heaven and run!

When I see a stripped-down wooden table, I can't imagine why anyone would want to buy it. But there are some people

> He restores my soul.
>
> Psalm 23:3

who can see past the current condition to a vision of what the table could be. They know that sanding it to make it smooth is a necessary process before it can be restained or painted.

It is much the same when the Lord begins to restore us after a time of hurt, loss, or sin. The Lord's sanding is important to our restoration process as He removes sins, behaviors, or anything else that hinders His purpose for our lives. It's in these times of sanding that we grow and learn to become more like Him. Are you in a time of sanding today? Ask the Lord to make you more like Him as He restores you.

"Therefore you also be ready, for the Son of Man is coming at an hour you do not expect."

Luke 12:40

Three things that really bug: a pop quiz; your parents walking in on you and your crush; the principal catching you without a hall pass. What do they all have in common? You're caught off guard. What could be worse than that? I'll tell you what. Being caught unprepared when Jesus comes back. Here's a question to ask yourself: If Jesus came back right now, would you feel OK doing what you're doing? If the answer is no, then you best beware.

EXTREME FOR JESUS

> "Which of you by worrying can add one cubit to his stature?"
> **Matthew 6:27**

I'm afraid of flying. So when I have to fly, I ask to sit by the window. It just seems safer when I can see what's going on. If you moved me to the aisle, I would worry and panic, because I couldn't see everything that was going on. The pilot just can't do it as well as if I'm not looking out the window, spotting any stray airplanes or high mountains. But is my worry really helping the plane to stay in the air? Of course not. If worry won't add any inches to my height, it certainly won't add safety to the plane I'm on. So why worry? Don't we trust God, the ultimate pilot? Can you trust God for everything? Is there something you are worrying about right now? Will you trust God to take care of it for you?

> ## We love Him because He first loved us.
> ### 1 John 4:19

Your bookcovers have his name all over them. You open your locker, and he's looking back at you from the photograph hanging on the door. You wear his letter jacket. You're in love. But how do you let your crush know that you care? Simple. You tell them. You talk with them, spend time with them, and write letters to them. You go places and just hang out. God wants to be your crush. He wants you to talk with Him, ask Him questions, and let Him talk to you. He wants to spend time with you and just hang out. And He has written a bunch of love letters—in His Word—for you to read. Show God that He is definitely your crush.

Nose. Tongue. Belly buttons. Rings and chains hanging from every possible part of the body. Tattoos embedded in the flesh. All in the name of fashion. Hey, that's not fashion. That's a cheap wind chime with a bad paint job. Not only has this become a part of to-day's culture, it's also become a major point of conflict in families. Here's the bottom line: If your parents would freak out if you came home with tattoos and piercings, then don't do it. If they're cool with it, then it's your choice. Call it rebellion. Call it self-expression. Call it what-ever you want. But until you get out on your own, you follow your parents' rules. Their au-thority was given to them by God.

> A wise son makes a glad father, but a foolish son is the grief of his mother.
>
> **Proverbs 10:1**

"Be very courageous to keep and to do all that is written in the Book of the Law of Moses."

Joshua 23:6

A team without a coach or playbook won't have a chance on the court. Have you ever felt like your life has no coach or playbook? Well it does. We've been given both. In fact, the coach shows up to every practice, to every game. He's on your side screaming for your win and shouting out plays. He can tell you how and when to dribble down the court, shoot a layup and score, or to just pass the ball. He promises you a big win if you just call Him coach. Are you tired of making up your own plays? Tired of being defeated by the other guys? Sign up for God's team, and let Him call the plays in your life.

"The LORD does not see as man sees; for man looks at the outward appearance, but the LORD looks at the heart."

1 Samuel 16:7

You are the best skateboarder in the area. No question about it. You can do moves on your board that no one else is even willing to attempt. Most of the people are in awe of you and your ability. Everyone sees that you were made to be a skateboarder. You give every event to the Lord, yet you still don't feel very close to Him. Competitions are on Sundays, so you don't go to church very often. Maybe that's the problem. Then it hits you. God isn't as concerned about your skateboarding as He is about you.

> As the deer pants for the water brooks, so pants my soul for You, O God.

`Psalm 42:1`

Have you ever been so hungry that you thought you'd die? After a long day of classes, practice, walking home? Your body is about to shrivel up and blow away. As you walk in the house, you smell fried chicken cooking, and you think you've died and gone to heaven. When you sit down to eat, every bite tastes like the best thing you've ever had. You're totally set. Life doesn't get any better than this. Well, that's what David meant when he said, "As a deer pants for water, so I pant for God." Has God ever been as good as a burger and fries when you're starving? If not, why not? Are you hungry for Him?

What if your faith was a new car? And what if the lordship of Jesus in your life was power steering and antilock brakes? When you bought that new car, would the power steering and brakes be options that you would

> "Go therefore and make disciples of all the nations."
> Matthew 28:19

pay additional money for, or would you think you could live without them? If you chose to save money and go without, then you might as well not even buy the car. If you say you're a Christian and you're not placing Jesus at the center of all your activity—striving daily to be just like Him—then your faith is useless. Jesus told His disciples to go and make others disciples. Disciples were the ones who were Christ's students. Studying His commands. Following His teachings. Are you a follower of Jesus or just a church-goer? Choose today what you will be.

As far as the east is from the west, so far has He removed our transgressions from us.

Psalm 103:12

Remember when you were born? Well, how about your first word? No? Why not? Oh, you were too young and can't remember that stuff. That's exactly the way God's forgiveness works. As soon as you ask God to forgive you, He does. If you come back to Him after being forgiven and ask, "God, remember that sin we were talking about yesterday?" God says, "What sin?" He doesn't remember it. It would be like asking you, "Do you remember when you ate your first meal?" Of course not. Even though God knows everything, He chooses to forget our sins. He's removed them from our record. How exciting! Ask God to forgive you, then let Him throw your sins in the trash, never to be remembered again.

EXTREME FOR JESUS

> My soul shall be joyful in my God; for He has clothed me with the garments of salvation.
> **Isaiah 61:10**

Jesus was cool with people. They liked Him. He was even invited to a huge party that became the place of His first recorded miracle. He was invited because they liked Him. He was cool to hang out with. Sure, He was on an important mission, but He liked to have fun. Being a Christian doesn't mean you have to be boring. It doesn't mean you have to turn into a Bible-thumping dork. Being a Christian is just the opposite of that. God promises that with salvation we'll have joy—joy that will make others want to be around us. Hey, you're loved by the Creator of the world. Get happy. Laugh. Smile. Have fun. Remember that being like Jesus means having joy.

> "Know that the LORD your God,
> He is God, the faithful God
> who keeps covenant and mercy
> for a thousand generations
> with those who love Him and
> keep His commandments."
>
> Deuteronomy 7:9

If you buy a dishwasher or a fridge, you might get a warranty. Most big things you buy require some kind of insurance. In case the thing breaks down after using it for awhile, the insurance allows a repair or replacement at no extra cost. But God's love doesn't require any kind of insurance, because there's no chance of it breaking down or springing a leak. God keeps His covenant—no insurance required. It's just pure *assurance*. In fact, His assurance lasts for a thousand generations. Even if you break it, He will still honor His end of the deal. It can never wear out, and it never needs to be replaced. Lifetime guaranteed.

It isn't a quiet faith that you have. Everyone who knows you knows where God stands in your life. He's the most important aspect of who you are. All decisions you make are with Him in mind. People find it encouraging to talk to you because you have such a warm and caring way about you. You speak from your heart about what God desires. You love to be with God as much as you possibly can, and it hurts to know that others sometimes won't find the time. Maybe they need help understanding how they can fall in love with a God they can't see. Help them obtain the same kind of love that no one questions. They probably need it.

> He said to him the third time, "Simon, son of Jonah, do you love Me?"
>
> John 21:17

"Observe all things that I have commanded you."

Matthew 28:20

Is there any way to be half a Christian? Can you pick and choose what stuff you agree with and what stuff you think is just too hard or stupid? Is it a smorgasbord—all you can eat and leave what you don't want for the next guy? Or is it a fine meal you've been invited to, where you have to eat whatever is served? Do you even know what all the "things that I have commanded you" are? It's hard to follow them and obey when you don't even know what they are. This week go through the Book of Matthew and make a list of all the things Jesus commanded you to do. The only way to be an extreme follower of Jesus is to follow in His footsteps. Strive to be just like Him and learn all that He commands.

He said to him, "Follow Me."
So he left all, rose up, and
followed Him.
Luke 5:27-28

"**D**isciple" is in the New Testament a whopping 269 times. "Christian" is in there 3 times. The word *Christian* seems to have lots of meanings. Most Americans claim to be Christians, but don't have a clue about being a disciple of Christ. A "disciple" was someone who left everything to follow Jesus. Anything less and they weren't disciples. Today we can't travel the countryside with Jesus, but we *can* be disciples by obeying Him and totally living the life He called His disciples to. Just like them, you will be a freak to some. But be tough. Living the faith may seem like a burden to unbelievers, but it's really the *freedom* of Jesus. Stop being controlled by the values of the world. Be set free by living like Christ's disciple.

> "And the LORD, He is the One
> who goes before you. He will
> be with you, He will not leave
> you nor forsake you."
>
> ## Deuteronomy 31:8

God is your Father. When you hear those words what do you think? "Great, so God is an alcoholic who beats up my mom." "God is going to walk out of my life when I need Him the most." "God is going to be too busy working to ever spend any time with me." Hey, God is perfect. He is your perfect Father. He'll guide you, and He'll protect you. He'll teach you, play with you, laugh with you, and cry with you. He'll do whatever it takes to make sure you have everything you need. He even promises that He'll never leave you or be mean to you. He's your perfect Dad. Thank God for being your loving Father. Go out and act in a way that will make your Father proud.

Weekend

The telephone rings. You hear, "Hello, my name is Rick and if I may take a moment of your time . . . blah, blah, blah." You would tell them no thanks if they would ever take a breath. But no.

"If anyone has ears to hear, let him hear!"

Mark 7:16

They keep yakkity-yakking. Do you think God ever feels like that? You call Him up and tell Him thanks for this or that. You ask for His forgiveness; you pray for a few friends. Then, "Amen," and you hang up. Hey! He wants to talk. The biggest reason people don't hear God is because *they* never stop talking to take time to listen. Today, give it a shot. Sit down with your Bible and a pen and paper. Focus on God . . . and listen. When you have a thought or feel something, write it down. It might be God finally getting the chance to talk.

> As He who called you is holy, you also be holy in all your conduct.
> 1 Peter 1:15

Imagine that you can observe your future husband or wife today. You can see them at school, at home, and even on their dates. How would you feel if their date's actions were less than godly? Would you be hurt by what you saw? Would you be angry at the other boy or girl? The truth is that, anytime you go out with someone, you are most likely dating someone else's future husband or wife. That person may very well be your future mate, but odds are, they're not. Treat those you date just as you would want someone else to treat your future husband or wife.

EXTREME FOR JESUS

> I will wait for the God of my salvation; my God will hear me.
> **Micah 7:7**

It feels like waiting for a ride that's running late? You pray and pray, but it seems God has hit a few stop lights or something. Isn't it frustrating when heaven's watch isn't on time with ours? Or so it seems. First of all, God is never late. That's N-E-V-E-R late. We just tend to be in a hurry sometimes. We have our schedules, our plans, *our* deadlines. Some of us have the cell phone mentality and wish God would go wireless, so He would answer us right now and in a hurry. He's listening. Just quit looking at the stopwatch. No land-speed records are broken in heaven. That's because God doesn't operate by our timetable. All He asks us to do is wait. He's on the job.

> "Seek first the kingdom of
> God and His righteousness,
> and all these things shall be
> added to you."

Matthew 6:33

Some people think it costs too much to pay cash, so they charge it—totally ignoring the fact that, in the end, they'll pay five times as much because of interest. They prefer the instant gratification of credit to the challenge of saving cash. But which price is actually higher? If you think that controlling your own life is easier than "paying the price" of living under Jesus' control, then you've missed some hidden costs. How much more would you gain by letting Jesus be your Lord, instead of your emotions? How much freedom would you have from worry, fear, rejection, or loneliness? Quit focusing on the cost of obeying Jesus and think about the high cost of not obeying.

Thursday

If you're on a soccer team you need a coach, someone who knows the game and can teach you how to play. If you're a singer you need a voice coach, someone who can sing and properly train you. To be successful at anything, you need someone who's been there before you—a coach. Do you have a spiritual coach? Someone older than you who can train you? A spiritual coach can encourage you, counsel you, listen to you, and pray for you. Think about someone whose faith you want in your life—someone you would love to be like. Ask them to coach you in the Christian faith. They will be honored you asked.

> If you instruct the brethren in these things, you will be a good minister of Jesus Christ, nourished in the words of faith.
>
> 1 Timothy 4:6

He stationed himself in the middle of the field, defended it, and killed the Philistines. So the LORD brought about a great victory.

2 Samuel 23:12

Where do you have to be on a regular basis? School? Job? Church? It may not seem like an important place, but it is to God. Shammah was in the middle of a pea patch, and he stood and fought. This was just a regular place. Nothing really special. But it was God's place. Shammah wasn't going to let someone mess with God's stuff. Look at the places you go. They may be regular places. But they may turn into battlegrounds. Sometimes you will be fighting for God in the middle of your daily life, and He will give you the power to win.

EXTREME FOR JESUS

Test all things; hold fast what is good.
1 Thessalonians 5:21

Ever had someone leave a message on your answering machine, "Hey, it's me, give me a call"? And you think, *Who on earth was that?* Sometimes we hear messages in our head, and we don't know if it's God speaking or just our mind thinking. When you think something is going on, but you don't know for sure, do this: Take whatever you're thinking about, whatever the deal is, and start looking for Scripture. Find as many verses as you can about that topic. See what the Word says. God will never tell you to do something that is against His Word. If what you hear fits with what the Word says, go for it! If not, you'll know it wasn't God.

What does the LORD require of you but to do justly, to love mercy, and to walk humbly with your God?

You just got a new computer game. You can't wait to load it onto your PC. That stupid "system error" message comes on the screen every time you try to load it, and you get very frustrated. You go back and read the box, and realize you don't have the correct system requirements. Ugh!! If you'd only known what the requirements were, the problems wouldn't have been there. Sometimes we don't realize what's required of us by God either. Is your life lining up with His requirements given you in this verse?

You go to church.

Why? Because everyone else expects you to, or because the Bible tells us to stay accountable to others through the "assembling of ourselves together"? You tithe. Why? Because it's expected of you—yet the whole time you're thinking about all the things you could've spent that money on? Or because you see that God is your provider, and the least you can give back to Him is ten percent?

God sees your heart, and He doesn't care about what it looks like on the outside. He cares about your motives. So why do you do the things you do? Are they just out of habit? Or is it because of love and a desire to serve God with all your heart? Think about it.

> All the ways of a man are pure in his own eyes, but the LORD weighs the spirits.
>
> **Proverbs 16:2**

"Do not fear, O My servant Jacob, and do not be dismayed, O Israel!"

Jeremiah 46:27

Have you noticed that God often starts speaking with, "Do not be afraid"? I'm sure hearing a voice from a bush or having an angel appear would be a shock. God can still shock us by having us believe there's nothing to fear in this crazy world. We can get scared so easily, but thankfully God wants to beat our fears—if we'll just ask Him. He knows that when our level of trust gets low, we're naturally going to be afraid. Where is your trust level? Will you trust God today?

> *Be still, and know that I am God.*
> **Psalm 46:10**

One guy doesn't know what to do, so he pleads with God to help him. He never stops asking God for help. He tells Him all his problems over and over. He still has no clue what to do. Another guy doesn't know what to do, so he asks God to help him. Then he sits still and waits for God to do and say the rest. Suddenly he's found the answer to his questions.

Which one do you want to be? Are you worrying instead of praying and listening? Are you revved up and forgetting that you have to shut up and let God talk? Spend time today in silence. Listen to Him.

Be anxious for nothing.

Philippians 4:6

Have you ever been totally embarrassed? Have you done something so stupid you don't think you can ever show your face again? How will you recover? Try not taking yourself so seriously. Other people get over it long before you do, so don't hang onto the shame. Repeating the episode over and over in your mind is worrying. Not ever going out again is fear. And both worry and fear are not cool for kids of God. Learn to laugh at yourself. And remember: The stupid stuff you do won't follow you around forever.

"Three . . . two . . . one . . . shoot!" The ball hits the back of the rim, bounces around, and pops out. Your team loses by one point. Major bummer. Disappointments are a part of life. But there's always more to the story. God allows us to be disappointed, but He doesn't leave us there. He wants you to see how much He loves you, and how He will take care of you. So the next time you're slapped in the face with a real downer, watch and see how God pulls you out of it.

> I want you to know, brethren, that the things which happened to me have actually turned out for the furtherance of the gospel.
>
> Philippians 1:12

Let nothing be done through selfish ambition or conceit, but in lowliness of mind let each esteem others better than himself. Let each of you look out not only for his own interests, but also for the interests of others.

Philippians 2:3-4

Your crush finally asked you out. You can't wait. Then . . . *bomb-out!* Your date is rude and can't talk about anything except what they've done or what they like. How could someone who seemed so cool be such a loser? If you want to know how to act on a date, check out the Word. Take an interest in what the other person is saying. Get to know them. Treat them better than you treat yourself. Then maybe that crush will be a match.

EXTREME FOR JESUS

No temptation has overtaken you except such as is common to man; but God is faithful, who will not allow you to be tempted beyond what you are able, but with the temptation will also make the way of escape, that you may be able to bear it.

1 Corinthians 10:13

You're in the middle of the best make-out session you've ever had with your "significant other." You're ready to go a little farther than just kissing when all of a sudden someone knocks on the door. If you answer, the moment will be over and you may never have this chance again— even though you know it's wrong. If you don't answer, you may end up doing something you'll later regret. God is providing a way out of the situation. Will you seize the opportunity?

> For all people walk each in the name of his god, but we will walk in the name of the LORD our God forever and ever.

Micah 4:5

What do you believe? That's a question asked a lot. In a world where so many different religions exist, the truth can become pretty muddy. One says he serves this god; another follows that one. It's like everyone has been given a treasure map, but not all of the maps lead to the treasure; an "x" may mark the spot, but there is no gold. They're searching for something that will not satisfy or save them.

Every day we walk in the name of God. Just like star athletes have brand-name endorsements, we have the endorsement of the power, love, and faithfulness of God. We represent Him, and He empowers us. It is the name of our God that gives us our salvation. We are walking in the power of His name.

Nathaniel was a little boy whose parents made him play in the backyard when they couldn't be outside with him to keep an eye on him. He didn't like playing in the backyard because it was fenced in, and that seemed like too much confinement. One day while he was playing outside, the fence took on a whole new meaning. On the other side of the fence was a rabid dog ready to tear Nathaniel limb from limb. He looked at the fence in a whole new light from that day forward.

> "Behold, happy is the man whom God corrects; therefore do not despise the chastening of the Almighty."
>
> Job 5:17

God's boundaries are protection for us also—not just a bunch of rules. He loves us so much and wants to protect us from harm and temptation. Today pray that God will help you to view His boundaries as safety from trouble.

"The LORD is in His holy temple. Let all the earth keep silence before Him."

Habakkuk 2:20

The radio. The TV. The Internet. So much noise and information all at once. How hard is it to hear God when you're listening to the world? Have you ever just sat alone in complete silence for more than five minutes? Scary thought, huh? What might you hear? Most people are afraid of silence because God might confront them. And they don't want that. They want to sweep a lot of pain and sin under the rug. But in silence you can't. It crawls out from under its hiding place, walks up to you, and stares you straight in the face. Only in the silence can you really grow and confront your fears, your enemies, and listen to your God. Try to go through part of your day in silence. Give God a chance to whisper through all the noise.

EXTREME FOR JESUS

"It is not the will of your Father who is in heaven that one of these . . . should perish."
Matthew 18:14

If you were on a boat and a guy fell overboard, would you reach behind you and get the life preserver to throw to him, or would you just go back to your seat and read your book? Pretty silly question, huh? Well, what if someone you know is drowning in life? What if their parents are divorcing or they're really depressed? What if they don't fit in, or they seem like a real jerk? Do you throw them a life preserver and pray for them? Or do you go back to your seat and read your book? Every day you have that choice. Every day you can choose to reach out to others and offer up prayers of protection, peace, love, and hope for them; or you can choose to turn away. What will you be today, a life preserver or just a book reader?

> A fool vents all his feelings,
> but a wise man holds
> them back.

Proverbs 29:11

Have you ever bumped your head? Yep, I thought so. Did it hurt? Uh huh. I thought so. We all learn early that two solid objects can't take up the same space at the same time without something getting hurt! So why try to take on the train of anger by standing in its way. When it hits, it's gonna hurt! Instead, move to the side. Try to see it from another point of view. Not only will you avoid being hit (with words of anger), but you'll be able to see the whole train instead of just the front!

Everybody has seen it. Your best friend leaves for their freshman year of college on fire and ready to win people to Christ. But the more you read their e-mails, the more you realize they're slowly backsliding. They went to train to preach, but instead they've embraced a bunch of "logical" blabber about evolution, everything being relative, and Buddha as a god, just in different form. Whoa! When they thought they were doing good by "expanding their horizons," they were really just getting empty knowledge to replace the godly wisdom they once had. Guard the truth. It's the only thing that will matter when you're standing in front of the throne of God.

> Guard what was committed to your trust, avoiding the profane and idle babblings and contradictions of what is falsely called knowledge—by professing it some have strayed concerning the faith.
>
> 1 Timothy 6:20-21

> Do not be conformed to this world.
>
> **Romans 12:2**

Magic. Illusions. Your eyes tell your brain that something happened, but your brain knows that it's impossible. But you're still mesmerized by the illusion. The world is full of illusions. The world tells us that we must use sex to get love, or witchcraft to get answers. It tells us we should use alcohol to get acceptance, or drugs to kill the pain. Hey, it's all an illusion. It's not the truth, but we're sucked into the magic of the moment and the thought of getting what we *think* we want. Be careful. There are a lot of traps out there. Look for the truth. Can the world really give you what you're looking for?

EXTREME FOR JESUS

> "Come aside by yourselves to a deserted place and rest a while."
> **Mark 6:31**

You're as busy as you've ever been, and it seems like everyone wants a piece of your time. Mom is on you that you aren't spending enough time with your family. Teachers are on you to finish your school projects. You have a lot of extracurricular activities that keep you busy—not to mention having a pager and a cell phone that make you available to everyone all the time. You often think about how nice it would be to have some time just for yourself. You think a lot at night because you're having trouble sleeping. Instead of thinking about taking a break, just go and take one. You might have to say no to some really cool things, but you'll refresh yourself and be better for it.

> "When you pray, do not use vain repetitions as the heathen do. For they think that they will be heard for their many words. . . . Your Father knows the things you have need of before you ask Him."

Matthew 6:7-8

Has a word ever been on the tip of your tongue? You know exactly what you want to say, but you just can't find the word? What is that? Thoughts without words? Don't they go hand in hand? It's been said that thoughts are always formed in the mind before they are ever spoken in words. If that's the case, can God understand us without the words? Can He read your heart? If so, then could you communicate with Him without words? Do you think He only gets it if you say it? How would your prayers change if you believed He knew what you needed before you even asked Him?

What would happen if one day you were on the practice field with no water? Let's say you're so thirsty that your tongue is starting to dry up. Then you spot a port-a-john just a few feet away. Would you go over and quench your thirst from

> Turn away my eyes from look-ing at worthless things.
>
> **Psalm 119:37**

its tank? Of course you wouldn't! Your sexual curiosity and desires can sometimes be just like that thirst. If you try and fulfill those desires with pornography, it's just like drinking from a port-a-john. Pornography is mental sewage that you'll never be able to get out of your mind. Wait for God's best in marriage.

Who is the man that fears the LORD? Him shall He teach in the way He chooses.

Psalm 25:12

God wants to have every part of our lives in His hands. He extends those hands to us every morning. Have you noticed? Does it scare you, those big hands coming at you? Is that what *fear* is? Actually, to fear God is to get the fact that He's holy, righteous, all-powerful, and all-knowing—and that we're weak, sinful, and needy. We would be totally powerless if He ever turned His face away from us. While fearing God doesn't mean being afraid of Him, our proper position should be facedown on the ground in total reverence and awe toward Him. How long since you've laid on your face in front of your Maker?

EXTREME FOR JESUS

> *God . . . gives us richly all things to enjoy.*
> ## 1 Timothy 6:17

Hurry up. Get movin'. We get so bored so easy. We gotta keep doing stuff. Do you really want to push the edge? You say you really want to experience God in new, exciting ways. Try this: Do nothing except to sit and listen. Listen to all the things that are going on around you—things you may have missed before. What do you hear? The air conditioner running? The refrigerator humming? The cars passing by? Birds chirping or dogs barking? We get so involved in what's going on in our little world that we forget about all the stuff going on around us. We're just a part of a big puzzle. Make yourself see and hear things you haven't seen or heard before. You'll be amazed at all the things in God's world you've missed.

> "Be strong and of good courage, do not fear nor be afraid of them; for the LORD your God, He is the One who goes with you. He will not leave you nor forsake you."

Deuteronomy 31:6

You're faced with a tough decision. This isn't like the time that you were dared to stand in a train tunnel as the train went by. That was easy by comparison, because that was just to show off. This has real life ramifications. You're now confronted with choosing a college. Money isn't the issue because of that trust fund from your grandpa, but you want to make a good choice. You're scared and you don't want to admit it, except to yourself. If you choose wrong, your whole life could be messed up. Mom and Dad say it's totally your decision. Where are you going to turn for advice?

Why do you do the Christian thing? Why do you go to church, study the Bible, obey the rules? There are four reasons to choose from, but only one is the right reason. People act Christian because 1. they've been told that's what they should do; 2. they want to make it to heaven; 3. they want to be different from the rest of the world; or 4. they love God. Why do you do what you do? If it's for any reason other than that you just totally love God, then eventually you'll find it all a real drag and give up on it. Obeying is really, really hard if you aren't doing it for the right reason. Think about it.

> Every way of a man is right in his own eyes, but the LORD weighs the hearts.
>
> **Proverbs 21:2**

> "Out of the abundance of the heart the mouth speaks."
>
> Matthew 12:34

You stub your toe. Out come the words. Your car doesn't start. Out come the words. Your life is a mess. Out come the words. You pray to God. Out come the words . . . out comes the heart.

Your mouth is essentially connected to your heart. Whatever is in your heart will come out of your mouth. It may be in a stressful time. It may be in a flood of anger, or just when you let your guard down. Whenever and for whatever reason, it *will* come out. Do a heart check and make sure that it is filled with godly desires. Whatever is there will eventually come out through your mouth.

EXTREME FOR JESUS

"Whoever humbles himself as this little child is the greatest in the kingdom of heaven."

Matthew 18:4

Popular. Great word. Don't you love being the center of attention? Getting all the credit, the trophies, the awards? It's nice to be recognized, huh? Addictive even. Do you ever search for ways to be noticed? And hurt when you aren't? God notices everything, so why do you try so hard to get people to notice you? Fame and recognition can do a lot for your ego, but can destroy your spirit. God wants you to forget being noticed and be humble. Blessed are the meek—remember? He's not looking for the most popular or the best. He wants you just as you are. This week try to find ways you can avoid getting credit for stuff. Do something for someone without telling anyone. Try to be anonymous. Give God all the glory.

> Thus says the LORD to you: "Do not be afraid nor dismayed because of this great multitude, for the battle is not yours, but God's."

2 Chronicles 20:15

The fact is, you're in a battle. In a battle you are losing if you're vulnerable or weak, exposed to attack, or without a way of escape. Fortunately, this is not a battle of flesh and blood, but rather a battle raging in the spirit realm. There's no need to fear when you know that God is in the fight. You can even read the end of the Book and see that He's already won the battle. No need to be afraid when you're on the side of the winner. How different then should you act knowing you're winning, not losing?

Little kids are so honest and so cute. A little six-year-old boy walked up to me and said, "Wow, you sure are tall to have such a little-bitty head." I just laughed and gave him a big hug. Now, let a 40-year-old or even a 16-year-old say that, and my reaction might have been a little different.

> Walk circumspectly, not as fools but as wise.
>
> Ephesians 5:15

The older we get and the more we learn, the more responsibility we have. As you grow up, you have more freedom, and with that freedom comes more responsibility. The more you grow as a Christian, you'll find out that you have more freedom. But you're also more responsible for your actions. Be careful what you do. There is always someone watching you. Are your actions drawing others to Christ or turning them away from Him?

The LORD is
near to those
who have a
broken heart,
and saves such
as have a con-
trite spirit.

Psalm 34:18

Crush. Why do we call them a crush? Because most of the time it feels like they threw our heart on the floor and stomped on it. You're not the only one. And it won't be the last time you get hurt. But remember, Jesus went through the same thing. One of His closest friends was a sellout and turned Him over to be killed. He walked through what you're feeling. Don't try to go through it alone. Talk to God. Yell, cry, get ticked, or whatever you need to do. He understands. He's been there. He also knows how to make the hurt go away. So listen to Him. He knows how to stop the hurt.

> Let each of you look out not only for his own interests, but also for the interests of others.
>
> ## Philippians 2:4

So you're ready to be radical for God? Then hang on because things could get a little bumpy. You've chosen the high road, not the low. It's a path few have traveled. Some people talk a good talk, but what about their walk? Being "Extreme for Jesus" means going all the way, not just talking about it. So here's the challenge: Today use all your energy to put someone else before yourself. Let them get in front of you in line. Let them take the credit for something. Do what they want to do, even if it's not fun. This is called self denial and it's not easy, but it is extreme. Will you put somebody else's needs before your own? Will you be radical for God?

EXTREME FOR JESUS

> Love ... thinks no evil.
>
> 1 Corinthians 13:4-5

I once had a friend who kept emotional postage stamps. Whenever someone would upset her, she would mentally lick a stamp and put it on a package in her mind. Over time, those stamps became enormous until one day, she would "mail" the package. She would blow up like a volcano—usually over some small thing—and dredge up all the things of the past she'd been storing. Have any friends like that? Or maybe that's you. Real love has an amazing ability to let go of stuff other people do to you. You may not be able to *mentally* forgive and forget, but you can emotionally. Choose today to let go of the things others have done to hurt you. Show them love instead.

Are you a child of the world? Do you buy what they tell you? Want what they tell you, because it's the real thing? When you watch TV this week, check out the commercials. How are the advertisers trying to tell

> Do not love the world or the things in the world.
>
> **1 John 2:15**

you how to think about yourself, your parents, your friends? How do they try to make you feel or act? What do TV shows tell us about God? About violence and witchcraft? How has TV taken wrong stuff and made it seem right? Always remember that you should not even desire anything unless it's in God's will. Don't let the world tell you what's right, because 9 times out of 10 they're wrong. Look through God-colored glasses and learn to pick out His stuff from theirs.

> Teach us to number our days, that we may gain a heart of wisdom.
>
> **Psalm 90:12**

It was one week before graduation as Michelle headed to a slumber party at her best friend's house. She rounded a corner, collided into an oncoming car, and was killed instantly. As our youth choir sang at her funeral, the reality that our days are numbered weighed heavily on us. I remember thinking that I wanted to live as though each day was my last. The Lord has given us the gift of life so we might know Him and give Him glory based on that knowledge. What are you doing with the days He's given to you? Do you desire to gain the wisdom of God so you can glorify Him today? If you knew that today was your last day on earth, what would you do differently?

EXTREME FOR JESUS

"These people draw near with their mouths and honor Me with their lips, but have removed their hearts far from Me, and their fear toward Me is taught by the commandment of men."

Isaiah 29:13

Two-faced. Back-stabber. Poser. You know who they are. People who say they're tight with you and then, as soon as you turn your back, they trash you. It hurts. It gets us crazy upset. That's who this verse is talking about—people who talk a good game about how they're really loving God, but what they say and do are totally opposite. God says it like we say it: "If you're gonna be My friend, do it. If you aren't—don't. Stop playing Me both ways." Do your words and actions focus on loving God? If not, watch out. Don't play God.

Imitate those who through faith and patience inherit the promises.

Hebrews 6:12

"**J**ust be patient," your mother tells you, "we'll leave soon enough." "Don't be too anxious to fall in love," your aunt says. Patience is a drag, huh? Having to wait is tough. How can a person be patient when there's so much to do? But without patience you can make some big mistakes—like rushing into bed with someone because you can't wait 'til marriage. Suddenly there's a baby on the way. Patience will help you in the long run, but how do you get patience? How about practicing at it, just like at anything else. Decide to get in the longest line and not to stress. Try to sit for five minutes and not worry about anything. Practice times like this will make you stronger. Soon enough you will have so much self-control, patience will be yours.

De-accumulate. That's the word for today. Give something away. Don't let things possess you when *you* possess *them*. If you have something you're afraid to give away, ask yourself if it's more important than God. Be careful not to put things before Him. He's jealous, remember. So go through your stuff and find something you can give away. It could be a sweater, a book, a CD. Find someone who's in need and give them something of yours. If you can conquer your need for things, you've conquered one of your enemies.

> "Beware of covetousness, for one's life does not consist in the abundance of the things he possesses."
>
> Luke 12:15

Pursue righ-
teousness,
godliness, faith,
love, patience,
gentleness.

1 Timothy 6:11

Any good fisherman knows that you don't use the same type of bait to catch a carp as you do a trout. The carp is a bottom dweller and the trout is a prize fish. Each are attracted by different types of bait. When you're seeking to attract your crush, the same principle applies. The things you use to attract the opposite sex will determine what type of person you get. If you attract them by using your body or your good looks, what do you think they'll be interested in? If you want to attract the right kind of person, you will need to display the right kind of qualities—righteousness, godliness, faith, etc.—to catch their attention. What qualities do you need to be building into your life to attract the right person?

Do not be envious of evil men, nor desire to be with them.

Proverbs 24:1

Who are the heroes of today? Actors and actresses? Musicians? Athletes? People can get a huge following today because they're "on the edge" or push moral limits. Think about what songs climb the charts, or what TV shows get high ratings. What about ads? Are we being fed a bunch of junk or what? God warns us that if we play with fire we're gonna get burned. We need to be careful not to just go along with what's popular or look up to someone who is ungodly. We need to look at the bigger picture and see if those we're looking up to glorify Christ or not. Who is your hero?

> The LORD said to Satan, "From
> where do you come?" So Satan
> answered the LORD and said,
> "From going to and fro on the
> earth, and from walking back
> and forth on it."

Job 1:7

Zeus. Medusa. Satan. All mythical figures who really don't exist. Right? Wrong! We aren't clueless enough to think Satan is just a mythical figure like the others. He's around alright. He and his army of demons are looking to destroy. They're searching for Christians that they can make turn away from God. Prepare yourself. Talk to God every day. Read the Word. Spend time with other Christians. Get ready and stay ready. Satan is looking for you to get weak so he can rip your faith apart. Get tough. Trust God to give you His power to stay true.

Tuesday

Rock climbing. What a rush! It's you against the rock. As you maneuver your way up the cliffs, you hook the rope you have tied to you into clips on the rock. Then if you fall, the clips and rope will stop you from falling—which would put a bummer into rock climbing. God's Word is our clip in life. It's what we should hook in to every day. If we fall, the Word will keep us from total failure. It will give us the security we need. It will even give us the surge we need to make it over life's obstacles. Get into the Word. Read it. Memorize it. It will save you from slipping and falling.

"Your words have upheld him who was stumbling, and you have strengthened the feeble knees."

Job 4:4

"When you fasted and mourned in the fifth and seventh months during those seventy years, did you really fast for Me— for Me?"

Zechariah 7:5

Sometimes we eat to cover up our pain or to make ourselves feel better. When we fast we say to our bodies, "You will not control me." We learn self-control. But when we fast we must always fast for God; otherwise it's a royal waste of time. In a rich country like ours, fasting often means more than giving up food. It's much more of a challenge. Fasting will also show us what controls us.

As you fast, problem areas in your life, such as pride and anger, can show up. In Bible days people fasted when they had something big to work out with God. They showed God that they really meant business. Do you have something that's worth fasting about?

EXTREME FOR JESUS

We are God's fellow workers.
1 Corinthians 3:9

So you say you've got this Christian thing down? You trust God. He takes care of everything; all you have to do is believe? You tell Him your needs, and off He goes to take care of it? Is it really that simple? Do you decide you need a job, so you ask God and then wait for someone to come to your door and hire you? Do you expect God to protect you so you don't buckle up? If Scripture is right—and it is—then that's wrong. We are to work alongside of God. We have to do our fair share. Don't expect to have wisdom without the Word. Don't expect to have strength given to you without constant prayer. Don't expect to win in the battles of life from your sofa. Get in and get your hands dirty alongside of God.

> "Do you suppose that I came to give peace on earth? I tell you, not at all, but rather division."

Luke 12:51

Christ came to bring us life, right? But He also came to bring division. Huh? Can it be true? See, believing in Him can cause division and conflict among the closest of friends and family. Some of your family will not understand why you're choosing to live your life for God. Some might even think it's stupid. How do you cope? Remember that it's more important what God thinks about you than what anybody else thinks. Your love for God might make love on earth difficult, but remember, He'll have all eternity to make it up to you.

You just got asked to be a part of the leadership team in your student ministry and you feel quite honored. After talking it over with your parents and examining the commitment, you accept. After one week of being involved, you have the chance to go rock climbing with some friends from school. The problem is, it conflicts with a major ministry event you're in charge of. You painfully come to the decision not to go rock climbing. Your friends just can't believe it. They can't believe that you would sacrifice rock climbing to do ministry. Sometimes doing ministry will mean sacrifice. What are you willing to sacrifice to serve Christ?

> For the work of Christ he came close to death, not regarding his life, to supply what was lacking in your service toward me.
>
> **Philippians 2:30**

So it was, when the Philistine arose and came and drew near to meet David, that David hurried and ran toward the army to meet the Philistine.

1 Samuel 17:48

Soccer is a sport of strategy. You must play good defense. But even if you have the best defense in the world, without any offense you'll never win a single game. You must attack the opponent. You know what the goal is. You must rage on, attack, and score to win. David was bold. He was playing the biggest and the baddest. But he attacked. No fear! He *ran* out to the fight. He didn't sit back. He attacked! He told the enemy exactly what he was going to do to him. And then he did it. When you have a major fight going on in your life, ask God to help you attack and conquer it!

EXTREME FOR JESUS

"It shall be, if you by any means forget the LORD your God, and follow other gods, and serve them and worship them, I testify against you this day that you shall surely perish."

Deuteronomy 8:19

What do you obsess about? What's hip and wearing the right clothes? Your car? Your computer? Basketball? What would you freak about if someone messed it up? We focus on things that could be destroyed at any time. Hey, whatever you obsess about, becomes a god to you. If you put the most energy and emotion into it, it controls you. Whatever controls you is your master. You are its slave. God's Word is straight-up: If you obsess about anything other than God, the payoff is death. Obsess about knowing God and His Word. He'll give you everything else you need.

> "Make yourself an ark of go-
> pherwood; make rooms in the
> ark, and cover it inside and
> outside with pitch."

Genesis 6:14

Imagine if God told you to build a giant spaceship in your backyard. "Make it the size of
five football fields, out of shiny metal, with really bright lights." "Excuse me, God? I don't
mean to sound rude, but what will I do with a
giant spaceship?" Can you imagine what your
friends and neighbors would say? The city
would probably shut you down—no permits for
spaceships. How hard would it be to follow
these instructions? Imagine how Noah must
have felt. But you notice what he did? He did
just what God said—even though it sounded
ridiculous. And look how it turned out. What is
God asking you to do that may seem ridiculous?
Will you do it?

"**G**o over and talk to those weird kids." "Tell your friends to stop teasing people." "Share your lunch with that loner." Has God ever asked you to do something that tough? Has He ever asked you to reach out to the untouchables?

> Jonah arose to flee to Tarshish from the presence of the LORD.
>
> Jonah 1:3

Wanna see what happens when you don't? Check out the story of Jonah. God told him to go talk to the whacked-out Ninevites, but Jonah thought that was stupid. So he split. And then chaos hit. The waves pounded, the boat rocked. Life was awful for Jonah, until what? Until he told God, "OK, I'll do it. I'll reach out to those oddballs—those ones who don't deserve You." Will you learn from Jonah and get it right the first time?

> "I saw the Lord sitting on a throne, high and lifted up, and the train of His robe filled the temple."
>
> Isaiah 6:1

When an actor came into town on Friday, it was a huge deal. Girls started screaming and crying when he got out of his limo. Seemed like they did everything but bow down and worship him. When the same girls came into church during the praise and worship service on Sunday, though, they looked like they might've had a better time at their uncle's funeral. They weren't impressed with the presence of God. No passion, no reverence, no worship. How it must sadden God, the Maker of the Universe! Our experience with the presence of God should bring humility, awe, reverence, and honor. We should be totally overwhelmed as mere people in the midst of a holy God.

EXTREME FOR JESUS

The LORD opened the mouth of the donkey, and she said to Balaam, "What have I done to you, that you have struck me these three times?"

Numbers 22:28

Donkeys were the SUVs of the day. They did it all. All of a sudden, Balaam's SUV started doing its own thing, and he got ticked and started beating her. Finally, the donkey had had enough and spoke up. That's right. The donkey said, "Listen, I'm saving your life and you're slapping me around. What's up with that?" See, the guy couldn't see the danger ahead. Things happen to us that seem to just get in our way. Our car won't start. We get lost. Our friend forgets to call. Instead of getting upset, thank God for protecting you. He could be keeping you from some kind of danger.

> "You are a holy people to the
> LORD your God, and the LORD
> has chosen you to be a people
> for Himself, a special treasure
> above all the peoples who are
> on the face of the earth."

Deuteronomy 14:2

"I'm worthless. Nobody likes me. I don't like myself. There's no way God can like me." Depression. Insecurity. We all feel like that sometimes. We feel like we're so alone, and the world would be better off if we weren't sucking up oxygen that someone else could be using. God knows that we get like this. But check it out. This verse says that we are His treasure. We were chosen. We didn't just fall into God's lap by accident. He has chosen us for Himself. He loves us and wants us to be happy.

Do you know what a spin-doctor is? He's like an ad man. He's usually someone who works for a politician and takes any issue and spins it to make his candidate look good. He makes everything look like his guy planned it that way, and things are all good. Did you know you had your own spin-doctor? Someone who takes everything that happens to you and makes it work out for your good? Well you do, and His name is God. Right now you might be going through major trauma. Life can't get any worse. But look out! Pretty soon God will come in and work it all out so you end up on top. Be patient and trust Him. He's good at what He does.

> We know that all things work together for good to those who love God.
>
> Romans 8:28

We have known
and believed
the love that
God has for us.
God is love.

1 John 4:16

"I love you." God says it. Do you believe it? Sometimes in the midst of the grind it can seem like God is nowhere. The fact that He loves you is just a distant memory, a story you heard one day in Sunday school. But right now you know it's true. Deep down you've always sensed it. He's been there through the good times and the bad. The hard part is how to re-member that. How about a love note from Him to you? Take a 3x5 card and write, "I love you" on it. Add a heart if you like. Sign it "God" if you want. But carry it around with you, tack it on your locker, carry it in your binder. Just never forget it—because He won't.

"As for you, if you walk before Me as your father David walked, and do according to all that I have commanded you, and if you keep My statutes and My judgments, then I will establish the throne of your kingdom."

2 Chronicles 7:17–18

It's hard to understand the difference between God's unconditional love and His conditional demands. God loves us no matter what we do to mess up. But He also puts really high expectations on our behavior—like seeking Him above everything else. He's created a life for us that works best when we follow His instructions. We think we know best, but God is going to continually prove to us that His way is the best way. God's way is the only way to experience all the blessings that He has to offer us. Which of His instructions do you need to follow more closely?

> Let each of us please his
> neighbor for his good, leading
> to edification.

Romans 15:2

Dising, joking, trashing, gossiping, roasting
. . . whatever we call it; does hurting
someone ever help them? We as Christians
aren't called to hurt people; we're called to
love them. So if we hurt people, can we really
call ourselves Christians? If we're gonna use
Christ's name, let's try to act like Him. Otherwise, we not only dis a person, but the Father,
Son, and Holy Spirit as well. That's a bad place
to be, don't you think? Today as you hang with
friends, remind yourself and them that if you
can't say anything cool don't say anything at
all.

Have you ever noticed that if you separate one of the embers from a bed of coals, it will quickly begin to get cold and dark? If you leave it with the other embers, though, it will stay hot and keep on glowing. Our spiritual walk is a lot like that ember. If we are around other Christians who are on fire for Christ, our spirits will continue to burn hot for God. But if we separate ourselves from those who are on fire, we will soon begin to grow cold in our faith and in our hearts. We need to go out and share our faith, but it is equally as important to surround ourselves with people who are on fire for God.

> As iron sharpens iron, so a man sharpens the countenance of his friend.
>
> **Proverbs 27:17**

"You also gave Your good Spirit to instruct them."

Nehemiah 9:20

God has put a bit of Himself into each of His followers. What a brilliant idea! His Spirit is in us—leading, guiding, and teaching. You might feel it in different ways. Some people might listen to their conscience; others might actually hear God talking to them or feel His gentle nudge. However you experience Him, the fact is that God wants to intimately involve Himself in your life. He wants your attention. The more you acknowledge Him, the more you'll get to know His voice. Can you feel Him leading you to reach out to someone who needs love? Can you hear Him suggesting that you repair a broken relationship? Are you responding to His direction?

EXTREME FOR JESUS

> "This commandment which I command you today is not too mysterious for you, nor is it far off."
>
> **Deuteronomy 30:11**

"OK class," your teacher says. "Today you will have a test that will determine your grade this semester." You freak. You didn't know there was a test today. The teacher says, "The question is, What color is the color blue?" You think there must be a catch. It's too easy. You answer the question *and* you get it right. God says that He is giving a test. We must follow His instructions. And He let's us know that it's not going to be rocket science. We already have the answer book. Read it, and you'll know the answers to life's questions. The Word of God has the answers. It's the answer book. Study the answers and you'll ace the test.

> Others had trial of mockings
> and scourgings, yes, and of
> chains and imprisonment. They
> were stoned, they were sawn
> in two, were tempted, were
> slain with the sword.
>
> Hebrews 11:36-37

Are there limits to how far you'll go for God? Is there some stuff that is just too extreme? Leaving your family for the mission field? Giving up a career for ministry? Fasting for a week to pray for a friend? How far is too far? Can God be pleased if we're only willing to go so far and no farther? Do you have a comfort zone where you stand with God? Have you ever thought of challenging it? Stepping out of the zone and into the light? What could you do today that would be out of your comfort zone? When you are extreme for Jesus life gets very exciting!

"**H**ey, what's your sign?" Do you ever open the magazine and turn to your horoscope? All your friends are doing it, so what's the harm? What about getting your palm read? Is there anything to that? They seem so right on. How do they know so much? The Bible tells us that we should stay away from that kind of stuff. They're playing with the spirit world outside of the will of God, and He doesn't want us to be messed up by them. So next time someone asks you what your sign is, tell them it's the Cross.

> "Give no regard to mediums and familiar spirits; do not seek after them."
>
> **Leviticus 19:31**

Blessed is he who considers the poor; the LORD will deliver him in time of trouble.

Psalm 41:1

As he held the sign that read, "Will work for food," many people passed him. Thoughts of trying to support his family stuck in the forefront of his mind. He just hoped that someone would give him the opportunity to work. Later that day a young man stopped and asked him if he knew how to do yard work. The needy man smiled and thanked God for the chance to take a meal home to his family that night.

God tells us that we have a responsibility to love our neighbor. Our neighbor is everyone, even that beggar on the corner. Christ chose to serve those in need. What choice will you make?

EXTREME FOR JESUS

The desire of the righteous will be granted. . . . The righteous has an everlasting foundation.

Proverbs 10:24-25

What on earth can we count on? Most would say, "Nothing." Fortunately, believers have a whole lot of "something" to count on in God's promises which have stood the test of time. Unfortunately, these promises don't take away the heartache. You will most likely have to go through some really hard stuff. But if you can remember the promises and hold onto them, you can never be completely destroyed. He even says the desires of the righteous will be granted, not like a genie granting three wishes, but like a potter who forms the clay. He will place the right desires in your heart as you allow Him to. Are you willing to let go of some of your own desires to make room in your heart for His desires for you?

> I will say of the LORD, "He is my refuge and my fortress; My God, in Him I will trust."

`Psalm 91:2`

The other night we had a tornado watch. Wind blowing. Trees bending. It was bad. The weatherman on TV said to go to the lowest part of the house and stay away from windows. I was scared. And I was worried because my cat was outside. I opened the door and yelled for him. But instead of running inside, he ran under the stairs and hid from me. As I crouched in the tub waiting for the storm to pass, I began to think about how many times I am too afraid of something to trust God. It seems too scary to let go of the control of some things. Hiding under the steps sometimes seems to be safer than risking running into His house. Run to Him. He has promised us safety and refuge when we do.

Tuesday

Are you afraid to ask for help? Do you think it's a sign of weakness to need help? Did you know that asking for help is actually a gift? Not a spiritual gift maybe, but people who can ask for help have been given a special gift from God. They've learned that they weren't made to do it alone. They've learned to be more Christlike. Jesus never did it alone. He was always getting advice and help from the Father and the Holy Spirit. He also had His disciples who were sent out to help preach the gospel. So don't ever think asking for help is a weakness. It's the way God planned it.

> God is our refuge and strength, a very present help in trouble.
>
> Psalm 46:1

Now Samson went to Gaza and saw a harlot there, and went in to her.

Judges 16:1

You're a Christian. You have a pretty solid walk with God. So it really doesn't matter who you date. You can date someone who isn't a Christian and you'll be able to change them. You're dating for Jesus. You know what? That's junk. You'll be taken into sin before you'll bring them out. You know the story of Samson and Delilah. He was set apart for God. She was into the world. But Samson thought he could handle it. That was the beginning of the end. Samson's life was destroyed because he chose to hook up with someone who didn't love Jesus. Be careful who you date. If they're not walking with Christ, then you don't need to be walking with them.

EXTREME FOR JESUS

> Warn those who are unruly, comfort the fainthearted, uphold the weak, be patient with all.
>
> ## 1 Thessalonians 5:14

Do you have friends who just get all over your nerves? They're great for short periods of time, but enough is enough. Chill! No one is perfect—not your family, your friends, or even you. If someone gets on your nerves, that doesn't give you a right to knock them in the head with your words and hurt them. Be patient. Be kind. Remember that God is perfect. You aren't. You may really get on His nerves. He doesn't just say, "Forget you." He loves you with all of your flaws. Next time someone is really getting to you, step back and think about how God sees them.

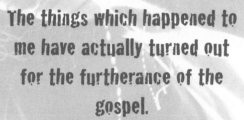

The things which happened to me have actually turned out for the furtherance of the gospel.

Philippians 1:12

A mother eagle has an interesting way of getting her young to leave the nest. When the time is right, the mother will begin to place thorns in the nest. She does this to make the nest uncomfortable so the young eaglets will leave. If she didn't do this, they would be tempted to stay in the comfort and shelter of the nest forever. God will sometimes do the same thing by letting hard stuff happen to us. These situations might hurt, but they help us grow and leave our comfort zones. Just as the eaglet has to leave the nest to soar, we have to leave our places of comfort to be the witness God wants us to be. If you're going through a difficult time, look for how God may be using this to help you grow and minister to others.

You love playing soccer; it's just the process of picking teams that you don't like. You're a good player; you just don't hang out with all the other soccer players away from the field. Most of them are into drinking and partying, and you have nothing in common with them other than soccer. In turn, you usually get picked last to be on someone's team. Even at that, they all act as if they have to settle for you, not that they really want you. The feeling of rejection is enormous, and you often walk away feeling hurt. It isn't based on your ability, only what you will and won't do off the field. Do you ever think God feels the same way?

> "They have not rejected you, but they have rejected Me, that I should not reign over them."
>
> 1 Samuel 8:7

"I will deliver them from all their dwelling places in which they have sinned, and will cleanse them. Then they shall be My people, and I will be their God."

Ezekiel 37:23

Even though God has set us free from the grip of sin, it seems that most times we prefer to stay in it. We get stuck in certain habits and get so used to the awful feelings of guilt and shame that they don't even bug us anymore. But God's asking you to walk away. He's giving you a way out. You don't have to figure this out; just accept it. Believe in faith that what God says is true, that He totally wants to forgive you of your sin. Will you believe it and act on it today?

EXTREME FOR JESUS

> Search me, O God, and know my heart; try me, and know my anxieties; and see if there is any wicked way in me, and lead me in the way everlasting.
>
> **Psalm 139:23–24**

It's 102° outside. You've been at the beach body surfing and playing sand volleyball all day. It's been a great day. You go back to your room to take a shower. OUCH! You are french-fried, extra crispy. Sunburned to the max. Then someone comes up to you, touches your back, and says, "Wow, does that hurt?" Pain shoots through your body. That's kinda like what happens when we spend a lot of time with Jesus, the Son of God. We become supersensitive to sin. Even the smallest touch of sin sends pain through us. So, do you want to know how to get away from sin? Spend more time in the Son.

> "The serpent deceived me, and
> I ate."
>
> Genesis 3:13

Has your brother or sister ever blamed you for something they did and you got in trouble for it? The blame game—we all play it. Guess who we got it from? The original parents: Adam and Eve. Remember them? God asks them if they ate the fruit, and they immediately pass the blame. Adam blames Eve. Eve blames the serpent. Why couldn't they just have been up front and honest? Human nature causes us to try to escape blame by putting it on someone else. But God isn't fooled. Don't blame anyone for your stuff. Accept the responsibility for things you've done.

Thursday

Is the Internet a gift from God or the devil? Does it help humanity or hurt it? How much time do you spend on-line each day? Has it replaced face-to-face contact with friends? Do you lock yourself in your room and stare at your screen all night? Do you think that's what God may have had in mind when He said not to give up hanging together as the pagans have done? Don't let your distractions occupy all of your time. They can easily crowd out your schoolwork, your family, and even God.

> All things are lawful for me, but all things are not helpful. All things are lawful for me, but I will not be brought under the power of any.
>
> 1 Corinthians 6:12

Bless those who persecute you; bless and do not curse.

Romans 12:14

Think of some ways that you bless people. To bless means that we desire God's best gifts for them and want them to be successful in all they do. We can bless others by praying for them or speaking kind, encouraging words to them or about them. Sometimes, it might require that we take action and go out of our way to help make them successful. This is a piece of cake when the person we're blessing loves us; but Paul says we are to bless our enemies. This seems quite extreme, and it's not easy, but as we rely on the Lord through prayer, He provides us with the strength to bless our enemies. What specific way will you ask the Lord to help you bless someone who has persecuted or hurt you?

EXTREME FOR JESUS

Jesus said to him, "Judas, are you betraying the Son of Man with a kiss?"

Luke 22:48

In today's terms Judas would be called a "sellout," because he betrayed his friend. Judas was a disciple of Jesus and saw Him perform miracles and love others like no one else before Him. But Judas turned his back on all that for a buck. Sounds stupid, huh? You'd probably never do anything like that, especially to Jesus, right? Turn your back on a friend? Every time we sin we turn our backs on God. It's like we think we know what's better for our lives than He does, so we betray Christ's leadership. Today make it your goal not to "sell out" on Christ!

> "Awake you who sleep, arise
> from the dead, and Christ will
> give you light."
>
> Ephesians 5:14

Waking up in the morning. There has to be a better process to go from asleep to awake. The waking up process bites. Being awake is cool. Being asleep is great. That whole middle part is just hazy. There are a lot of Christians living their life in that zone. They say they're Christian and they're awake, but they really don't live extreme for Christ. They're not stretching and learning. They're in that middle that really bites. If you say you're going to live for Christ, live it. If not, get outta the way. You may be causing more damage than good.

Breaking up is hard to do. Especially with someone you really care about. But sometimes you know you have to do it. Other times you're the one getting dumped. When someone hurts you, you could be totally tempted to dog them to your friends. You could tell everyone how they did you wrong. Why not

> Let all bitterness, wrath, anger, clamor, and evil speaking be put away from you, with all malice.
>
> Ephesians 4:31

step up and choose to live to the extreme? How can you do that? Don't go the way of bitterness. Stop being angry. Say good things about the other person. No, it won't be easy, but it'll be what God asks you to do.

Let no corrupt word proceed out of your mouth, but what is good for necessary edification.

Ephesians 4:29

You log into the chat room. You check out who's there. You say hey. The talk begins. You tell them about this guy, who you think's a real geek. You have to get it out, and besides these chatters live three states away or more. What harm could it do? Does gossip no longer count when it's typed instead of spoken? Was God surprised by the invention of chat rooms? Is that why they aren't mentioned in the Bible? Talking about people isn't cool. Even when it seems safe. So only say something if it's good. Avoid the petty stuff.

You are our epistle written in our hearts, known and read by all men.

2 Corinthians 3:2

Have you ever gotten a love note? How did it make you feel? It's a rush, huh? To know someone really likes you is so cool. An epistle is a note, or a letter, written in Bible days. Paul was telling the Corinthians that they were a love note written by Christ Himself. In the same way that the Bible is a love note from God, you yourself are a love note written by Jesus. Your life and everything you do is a letter for all the world to read. What will the world read from your life?

EXTREME FOR JESUS

> "It shall come to pass that before they call, I will answer; and while they are still speaking, I will hear."
>
> Isaiah 65:24

Imagine pulling up to a fast-food drive-through. Before you start ordering the person says, "Sure, one hamburger coming up." You knew you wanted to order that, but you hadn't told the person inside. Then just when you're about to tell them to hold the pickles . . . "No problem; we won't put any pickles on it." OK, now you're starting to get a little freaked out. It's doubtful this will happen at a drive-through, but with God it happens all the time. What does this mean about prayer? It means you don't have to try so hard to express yourself to Him. He already knows your needs. Just spend time in His presence. Think about Him. Come before Him, and don't worry about what to say.

We can be so quick to point out how other people don't deserve the things they think they do, all the while thinking we *do* deserve things that we actually *don't*. The truth is, we get more than we deserve—especially when it comes to God's forgiveness. If you compare it with how much forgiveness you've been given, there's no limit to how much you can dish out. The only time you can't forgive someone is when you start to believe that the forgiveness you've been given is something you *deserve*. Will you forgive others as much as you've been forgiven?

> Peter came to Him and said, "Lord, how often shall my brother sin against me, and I forgive him?"
>
> Matthew 18:21

Be kind to one another, tenderhearted, forgiving one another, even as God in Christ forgave you.

Ephesians 4:32

They found the remains of over 15 young people in his apartment. Pictures and video tapes of tortures. Bodies and parts of bodies were kept like trophies. The guy was convicted of capital murder and forced to stand before the families of his victims. News stations carried the event nationwide as parents, brothers, and sisters stood and shouted everything imaginable at him. Rage. Hate. Bitterness. Then one last man, a victim's father, stood and said something unbelievable: "Today I will begin to forgive you. I will not allow you to murder me with my hate." Then he sat down. Forgiveness. Try it.

EXTREME FOR JESUS

Some trust in chariots, and some in horses, but we will remember the name of the LORD our God.

Psalm 20:7

Two guys got into a fight. They went outside and one guy pulled out a knife. The other guy started laughing hysterically. Sorta freaked out, the guy said, "What are you laughing at?" The other guy stopped laughing and said, "What kind of idiot would bring a knife to a gun fight?" Then he pulled out his gun and shot the dude. Listen, there is always someone bigger, badder, or better than we are. If we put our trust in what we can do, we will lose. Trust in God your Father. Trust that He will take care of you in little things and big things.

> We are hard-pressed on every side, yet not crushed; we are perplexed, but not in despair; persecuted, but not forsaken; struck down, but not destroyed.

2 Corinthians 4:8-9

Have you ever felt like a soccer ball, beaten up, crushed, thrown around? You're worn out. Tired of the fight. You're not alone. The apostle Paul felt the same way. But look how he responded: "struck down, but not destroyed." He knew that the Enemy hadn't beat him to the point of giving up, so he was still winning. If you've given up, the Enemy has already won. But as long as you don't give up, you're winning. When the Enemy tries to score one on you, say this verse out loud. Let him know you aren't a quitter.

Do you ever watch "Touched by an Angel" and think, "Man, I wish I had an angel hangin' out with me!"? Well wish no more, 'cause you do. Even though you can't see them, they're there. There's a whole world going on around us that we can't see. Angels protect God's chosen— you—from the schemes of the Enemy. You play a part in this battle when you pray to God for strength for your friends, family, and yourself. God enlists His troops to fight the battles alongside you. So never feel alone in the fight. There's always someone there with you.

> The angel of the LORD encamps all around those who fear Him, and delivers them.
>
> Psalm 34:7

> "You shall receive power when the Holy Spirit has come upon you; and you shall be witnesses to Me."
>
> Acts 1:8

Check this out. Take a nuclear-powered submarine and put it in a pond. What a total waste of energy—all that potential just to turn lily pads into launch pads.

Take the awesome power of the gospel of Jesus Christ and let it motivate you. We have a surging power plant in us to reach the world with God's message of love. Why wouldn't you take advantage of all that energy? Just like the sub wasn't intended for a pond, we were not intended for silence. Make the message known. Use that power inside you to help break the grip of sin in people's lives. Don't waste it.

Humble yourselves under the mighty hand of God, that He may exalt you in due time.

1 Peter 5:6

You're in art class working on a group project with your friend. You come up with the idea of using the talents of the class to paint several murals around the school. Your friend comes up with a few designs and you show your teacher. The teacher loves the idea, and your friend starts to really run with the project. The school gets painted and your friend gets all the attention, while you sit in the background with very hurt feelings. After all, it was *your* idea. They just ran with it to make it happen. How often are you confronted with wanting to exalt yourself? It's easy to fall into that trap, but remember: God knows what you've accomplished. He won't let it slip by.

> Jonathan spoke well of David to Saul his father, and said to him, "Let not the king sin against his servant, against David."
>
> 1 Samuel 19:4

Jonathan and David had a very cool relationship. Their total commitment is a great example of true friendship. Jonathan's dad was on the rampage against David, so he decided to help David by talking to his dad for him. Anytime we choose to say nice things about our friends to other people, we're imitating this relationship. Instead of joining in the conversation the next time you hear people cutting someone down, try to stand up for them. Maybe you can change the way some people think. Are you willing to stand up for others? Is there anyone you think would be willing to defend you to other people?

I know you weren't expecting to have to write anything down. But get a pen and paper. Make a list. What does a godly person look like? How does he talk? How does she dress? What do they do? Make a short list of what a Christian looks like. Now, look at the list. Do you look like this? Where are you off? Work on that today. Work on the list until you look like what a godly person looks like. You were created in God's image. Isn't it time you started looking like Him?

> God created man in His own image; in the image of God He created him; male and female He created them.
>
> Genesis 1:27

"Take now your son, your only son Isaac, whom you love, and go to the land of Moriah, and offer him there as a burnt offering."

Genesis 22:2

Do you have an Isaac? Something God wants you to give up? God never meant for Abraham to kill Isaac; He was just testing his faith. When God asks you to put something on the altar, it isn't easy. It will be something you love. If you have something you love more than God, be prepared to sacrifice it. If it's in God's will, He'll give it back. Holding on too tightly to anything in this world is out of God's will. What is He asking you to give up?

EXTREME FOR JESUS

"Now I know that you fear God, since you have not withheld your son, your only son, from Me."

Genesis 22:12

Yesterday you read about sacrifice. Have you given it any thought? Is there something you just won't let go of, even for God? If there is, then you have yourself an idol. That's right. You obviously fear losing your idol more than you fear God. Why don't you just make up your mind and give it to God? Write it down on a piece of paper, stick it in the fireplace, and burn it. Or flush it down the toilet. Show God that you're ready to lay your Isaac down on the altar, even if it means losing it forever. Show God how much you love Him.

> Submit to God. Resist the devil and he will flee from you. Draw near to God and He will draw near to you.
>
> James 4:7-8

There was once a worn-out Bible teacher who had a class of whiny Christians. "I can't seem to stay pure . . . I can't pull out of my depression . . . I always give in to peer pressure." So one day, after hearing this for hours, the teacher gets totally frustrated by their lack of response to his help. Slowly he gets out of his chair, grabs his briefcase, starts out the door, and says softly, with his eyes closed, "Give in to God. Stay away from the devil, and he'll stay away from you. Get close to God, and He'll get close to you. Good-bye." This is how God must feel about us sometimes—especially when the answers are right there in front of us.

It's almost more than you feel you can bear. Mom and dad took you out to dinner tonight to tell you that they're getting divorced. Why? They always seemed happy together, but now they say they feel as though

> Casting all your care upon Him, for He cares for you.
>
> 1 Peter 5:7

they've drifted apart. You're devastated and feel like you're going to throw up at any time. You know the verse in the Bible that says to cast your cares on God. Right now, however, it feels like the words are just *blah, blah, blah*. You wonder what it really means to give God your anxiety. Why don't you tell Him that and ask Him how to do it?

David said, "Is there still anyone who is left of the house of Saul, that I may show him kindness for Jonathan's sake?"

2 Samuel 9:1

Because of Jonathan and David's tight friendship, David had really wanted to help out all of Jonathan's relatives after Jonathan was killed. This idea of helping people's extended family is a great way to carry a friendship beyond death. Is it possible for you to develop such a close friendship right now that you would be there for your friend's kids or grandkids years down the road? What would that take? How far into the future will your love for your friends carry on?

EXTREME FOR JESUS

> You shall call, and the LORD will answer; you shall cry, and He will say, "Here I am."
>
> ## Isaiah 58:9

What if God had an answering machine? Wouldn't that bite? Playing phone tag with the Creator when you wanted to talk with Him. He doesn't. Thank God. No, really. Thank God that He doesn't have a machine, call waiting, call blocking or any of that. When you call His name, He answers. You don't have to wait. He even answers before you finish His name. Call Him today. Tell Him what's up in your life. Tell Him what's going smooth and where you need help. He's there; where are you?

> "Woe to you Pharisees! For you tithe mint and rue and all manner of herbs, and pass by justice and the love of God."

Luke 11:42

Do you have a five-minute faith, only giving God five minutes a day? Is it enough? What if God only gave *you* five minutes of *His* day? Would that be enough? The Bible says we are to give God the first and best of our stuff. It says to give Him the top 10% of it. What if your most important stuff is your time? Can you give Him 10%? What is so important that you don't have time for God? Plan today to spend more time with Him. When can you do that? How can you arrange it?

Thursday

The city bus stops. An old man slowly climbs the stairs and walks down the isle. All the seats are taken, so the man feebly reaches for the pole to hold himself up as the bus jerks to take off. To his right a couple of businessmen sit with their faces buried in the newspaper. To his left a couple of teenagers joke and laugh. All of them have energy to bounce down the isle and out the door, but yet they don't move when the man comes in. Is God happy? Is the man honored? Is God honored? What would you do?

"You shall rise before the gray headed and honor the presence of an old man."

Leviticus 19:32

"What man is there among you who, if his son asks for bread, will give him a stone? Or if he asks for a fish, will he give him a serpent?"

Matthew 7:9-10

"Dad, can I eat? I'm so hungry. Please give me some bread." Just then a plate of rocks appears at your feet. Huh? "I'm cold. Can I get a blanket?" A snake curls up next to you. What? Can you imagine a dad doing something like this? Then why would we think God would do it? When you ask God for something, you don't have to be afraid of what He'll give you. He promises that it's going to be His very best, even if it doesn't seem like it at the time. He knows your needs; He gave them to you. So don't be afraid to ask Him for things. He loves you too much to give you anything but the best.

EXTREME FOR JESUS

> "Whoever looks at a woman to lust for her has already committed adultery with her in his heart."
> **Matthew 5:28**

Most of a guy's sexual temptation will come from what he sees. Advertisers know about this strong visual stimulation to sexual attraction, and they exploit it to sell everything from beer to shampoo. Many girls also use this visual attraction to get the attention they want. Guys, if you're going to remain sexually pure both physically and mentally, you have to guard what your eyes look at. You can sin sexually without even laying a hand on the girl. Girls, you also have a part in this. Knowing that the visual stimulation causes such great sexual temptation for guys, how should you dress and act around them?

> The king said to Barzillai,
> "Come across with me, and I
> will provide for you while you
> are with me in Jerusalem."
>
> 2 Samuel 19:33

Many people have a limit on how much they will do for another person. We'll only go so far until we expect to get something in return for all our efforts. If you have a friend, you should be committed to doing whatever you can to help meet their needs. The church body is designed to be God's hands and feet, working on living out His will on Earth—something that can only be done as we continually act in love and compassion toward other people. God doesn't set limits on how much He cares for you. Why should you?

Tuesday

You decide to get a dog, even though you live in the middle of the city. Where will you keep him? Do you just throw the dog outside where he could get hit by a car or caught by the dogcatcher? No way. You put him inside a fence because you want him to be protected. Look at the rules you have to follow as a fence that protects you from bad things. If you stay inside the rules—stay inside the fence—you're protected. But if you get outside the fence . . . watch out! Be happy that God is protecting and guarding your life with His rules.

> Take firm hold of instruction, do not let go; keep her, for she is your life.
>
> Proverbs 4:13

> "You shall not glean your vineyard, nor shall you gather every grape of your vineyard; you shall leave them for the poor and the stranger."
>
> Leviticus 19:10

Do you get an allowance? Do you have things? Clothes, stuff? Ever think of sharing it? I mean giving it away. Are there other people in this world who have less than you? Other kids who would love to have a warm meal in their stomachs? How can you share with them? You think you're too young? Think again. You're never too young to be used by God to help others. Show the world that your generation isn't selfish. Think about others. Give. Follow God's command—even if it seems like it's for adults only—and watch what God does with your life.

EXTREME FOR JESUS

> "Everyone who curses his father or his mother shall surely be put to death."
> **Leviticus 20:9**

Aren't you glad you didn't live in Old Testament days? Would you have been put to death? I know I would have. It's so hard *not* to "curse" your parents. Sometimes they just seem so clueless. You know they'll love you no matter what, so it's easy to get mad at them—easier, in fact, than it is with anyone else. But God made a pretty big statement when He said you'd be put to death for smart-mouthing them. God doesn't do mouthy kids. Don't tick God off. Give your parents some respect—the respect that God demands.

> He made Him who knew no sin
> to be sin for us, that we might
> become the righteousness of
> God in Him.

2 Corinthians 5:21

It's not just a *car* you want; you want a four-wheel drive and not just any four-wheel drive—you want a Hummer. It's beyond transportation; it's status. You don't want to just date; you want to date the person your friends feel is the ultimate. It isn't about dating; it's about who you are seen with. You know what? God doesn't care. You can't drive enough cool cars, date enough beautiful people, have the best grades, or do anything else to impress God. Fortunately, He isn't as concerned with that stuff as we are. What God is concerned about is your understanding of Him and what He did for you. Do you know what that is?

Whoa! Can you imagine how cool it would be to know more than all your teachers? You can get there by meditating on God's Word. But what in the world is "meditation"? That just means to think about what you've read. God didn't give us the Bible just to carry to church. He wants us to read it. And

> I have more understanding than all my teachers, for Your testimonies are my meditation.
>
> Psalm 119:99

He wants us to focus on what we've read—to think about it over and over again. It has all kinds of stories about people who had to make some tough choices. And you know what? They didn't always make the right choices either. Some had successes because they listened to God. Some had failures because they didn't. Pick up the Book. Read it. Listen to God. Then learn to take direction from Him. That's what it's all about.

> "He who is not with Me is against Me, and he who does not gather with Me scatters abroad."
>
> Matthew 12:30

You may say, "I run my own life. No one controls me. I make my own decisions." Whatever! The Scripture is clear. You either live your life for God or Satan. Living it for yourself is not an option. Two teams are playing basketball. You can only play on one team. Two sides are competing for your life. If you're living for anything except God, it's for Satan. It's your choice which side you're on. Choose to live for God. Be on His team. Read His playbook called the Bible. Then you'll be playing to win.

But as we have been approved by God to be entrusted with the gospel, even so we speak, not as pleasing men, but God who tests our hearts.

1 Thessalonians 2:4

"Hey, go stick your tongue on that frozen pole," the kids shouted at me. "If you were tough enough you would." Can you say S-T-U-P-I-D!? I couldn't. My tongue was stuck to the flagpole. Every day people will try to get us to do some stupid things—some more stupid than others. But remember: We are not trying to make others happy, just God. Listen to Him and do what He wants you to do. Otherwise, you might find yourself kissing a flagpole.

EXTREME FOR JESUS

> The hypocrite with his mouth
> destroys his neighbor.
> **Proverbs 11:9**

Do you ever say one thing and do another? Do you tell everyone how much you love God and then spend two hours talking about your ex? Do you go to Sunday school one day and watch a not-so-Christian movie the next day? Do people know what to expect from you? Are you consistent? Do you treat one kid different from another kid because of how they look? Have you ever been called a hypocrite? Seems like something someone else is, but not you. If how you talk and how you act don't line up, then you *are* one.

Have you heard of the kid who cried wolf? He played around and played around so many times that when the wolf finally came no one believed him. Do people believe you when you speak? When you say you will be somewhere at 5:00, do they know that means 5:15 or 5:30 to you? Do your words match your actions? Can people trust you? You might not think being late has anything to do with having integrity, but if you can't be trusted to even show up on time, then when can you be trusted? Watch your actions today, and see if they track with your words.

> Better is the poor who walks in his integrity than one who is perverse in his lips, and is a fool.
>
> **Proverbs 19:1**

> For where envy and self-seeking exist, confusion and every evil thing are there.
>
> James 3:16

You think it's just a little envy—that's all. It's no big deal. Think about swimming in the ocean with a small cut on your finger. No big deal? Well, it is for the sharks that can smell blood from a mile away.

Envy may not seem very threatening in today's world. But what we don't realize is that, when it makes it's way into our relationships, it opens the door for other damaging emotions like unforgiveness, bitterness, and hatred. There's no gain worth the pain of envy. Keep your attitude focused on God.

> Let us lay aside every weight, and the sin which so easily ensnares us.
> **Hebrews 12:1**

"Danger. Riptide. Undertow. Beware! Ocean is rough." A riptide is a current of water below the surface that will slowly drag you away from the shore—so far that you can't get back. Many unsuspecting swimmers have slowly drifted to their deaths by this phenomenon. If you're not careful, sin can do the same thing in your life. It's easy to let "small" sins enter your life by saying, "It won't really hurt anybody." The truth is, any sin will draw you away from fellowship with God. Before you know it, you'll find yourself far away from God wondering how you ever got to that point. Guard against even the so-called small sins, because they'll slowly pull you away from God.

> Obey those who rule over you,
> and be submissive, for they
> watch out for your souls.
>
> **Hebrews 13:17**

God has put people in positions of authority. We may think they're idiots and not capable of being good leaders, but it's not our job to question their authority. We have been commanded to do what they say. That means stop giving your teacher a hard time. Yes, that even includes the substitute teacher. Your parents, coach, the police—they're all authorities. Do what they say. Not because they say so, but because God's Word says so.

Beepers, cell phones, faxes, e-mail, Internet. We are wired. Gotta be connected. And not just connected—but digital. What are you connected to? Get the hookup. Connect with other Christian friends. Plug in to a Bible study and a church that fits your style. Spend time alone with God. Just you and Him. Christ is all about showing you His love. So you gotta get wired to Him.

> To know the love of Christ which passes knowledge; that you may be filled with all the fullness of God.
>
> **Ephesians 3:19**

I will set nothing wicked before my eyes.

Psalm 101:3

How much does it kill you not to be able to see the movies your friends do? How left out are you? Do you wish you could go just this once to that scary movie? It's so not real, all that bloody-knife, stab-'em-in-the-face stuff. How could it hurt? It's just a movie. Whether you realize it or not, it affects you. Satan has gotten very good at desensitizing us to sin. These movies with all the violence and sex affect the way we look at life. Life becomes not so sacred, not so holy anymore. Each step takes us further away from God and closer to the Enemy. So keep wicked things from your eyes.

EXTREME FOR JESUS

Love suffers long and is kind.
1 Corinthians 13:4

The Bible says that God is love. So if God is love, then what happens if we substitute the word "God" in the place of "love." "God suffers long and is kind." Did you know that about God? "Suffers long" means He never gives up. He puts up with it all. He put up with David sleeping with another man's wife. He put up with Peter denying Him—three times. He puts up with you and all your mess-ups. Don't ever worry that you've messed up too much for God, because you can't. He loves you too much. So much, in fact, that He *is* love.

> Be my strong refuge, to
> which I may resort continually;
> You have given the command-
> ment to save me, for You are
> my rock and fortress.

`Psalm 71:3`

There was a fire in the barn. The farmer was worried about the new chicks that had hatched the day before. After the fire had been put out, the farmer quickly went into what was left of the badly burned barn. His heart sank as he approached the nest where the chicks lay. The mother hen lay in the nest burnt and lifeless. The farmer picked up the hen, and to his surprise all the chicks were alive. The mother hen had died protecting her own.

As Christians, God is our protector. He's our shelter in life's storms and fires. He loved us so much that He sacrificed His Son that we might live! Make it your prayer to thank God for His protection!

When I was little, my brothers and I would take towels and fasten them around our necks as capes—which instantly transformed us from children into amazing superheroes who could run fast, and save stuffed animals and our whole household from invaders. When we as weak humans decide to put on Christ, or to clothe ourselves with Him, we choose to put on His character. We dress in His superpowers of love, humility, grace, mercy, and strength. It is through these pieces of clothing, that we're able to become superheroes for Christ. His life transforms us as His power equips us to live for Him, while denying our own sinful natures. What are you wearing today? Does your clothing reflect the character of Christ?

> Put on the Lord Jesus Christ, and make no provision for the flesh, to fulfill its lusts.
>
> **Romans 13:14**

"Come to Me, all you who labor and are heavy laden, and I will give you rest."

Matthew 11:28

It's easy to find all sorts of mind-numbing stress relievers today. Some people look to drugs or alcohol to help them through their traumas. Others turn to their hobbies, friends, music, or TV. Some even go to all kinds of church activities to find relief. Do you know what God's remedy for stress-relief is? He says, "Come to Me!" Don't keep running to the stuff of the world. It's just counterfeit. Oh, yeah, it might help numb your pain for awhile, but eventually it will leave you feeling just as empty and defeated as the trauma has. Go to Jesus. He promises to give you rest.

EXTREME FOR JESUS

Blessed is the man who walks not in the counsel of the ungodly, nor stands in the path of sinners, nor sits in the seat of the scornful.

Psalm 1:1

The party is Friday night. It will be the *BOMB* of the year. Whatever your party pleasure is, it will be there—booze, smoke, sex, whatever. Now that's not your game, but you *are* into being at the party. You will go and just not mess with that stuff. After all, you're a Christian. Listen, you're putting yourself in a situation that you shouldn't be in. You could get into big trouble, or even get hurt. Step back, get real with yourself, and find something else to do.

Love does not envy.

1 Corinthians 13:4

"Envy" means to grudge another person's fortune. You have a friend who has a shiny, new convertible. Do you envy them? Wish it were yours? Complain about being too poor for such a nice thing as that? You have a friend who gets better grades than you. Do you just wish that one day he would get a D, or even a C? You envy them. Envy has nothing to do with love. If you want to learn to love, then don't be upset because your friends succeed where you don't. Cheer them on. Be happy for them. In the end, you will have your reward in heaven.

When you have on the newest, hottest pair of shoes, does your walk turn into a strut? Do you just hope and pray that everyone is looking so they can see how cool you are? Do you show off in front of all your friends? If you do, then you don't know what love is. Ask God today to teach you more about love. Because, without love, we are nothing more than a really loud, really obnoxious drum set being played by someone who has no idea what they're doing.

> Love does not parade itself, is not puffed up; does not behave rudely, does not seek its own.
>
> 1 Corinthians 13:4-5

When He came to the place, He said to them, "Pray that you may not enter into temptation."

Luke 22:40

Praying the first thing in the morning is like tying your shoes before you begin a long walk. If you tie them well, your walk is easy. If you don't, then you'll trip up along the way. Your shoes will flip-flop all over the place. You'll stumble. Then . . . WHAM! You may even end up tasting the pavement. Now, this might be funny for everyone around you, but it's embarrassing, and just plain stupid. Take a little time, and get your shoes tied the right way. Pray!

EXTREME FOR JESUS

Do not be carried about with various and strange doctrines.
Hebrews 13:9

It sounds pretty good—"God helps those who help themselves." You know it's in the Bible because you've heard it quoted from the Book of Hezekiah. You bring it up at the latest Bible study that you're having, only to get waxed by most everyone there. After a short investigation, you discover that not only is that verse not in the Bible, but there is no such book as Hezekiah. It sounded so good and biblical, when in reality it isn't even there and you got dooped. It gives you a new understanding of those people who get involved in cults. They get a nice, feel-good quote, but it isn't represented in Scripture. It also helps you realize that you can't take your knowledge for granted. How solid is your grasp of what you know about God?

> What man can live and not see death? Can he deliver his life from the power of the grave?

Psalm 89:48

There's no question that we'll all die. There is a question about *when* we'll die. But that's one that only God knows the answer to. What would you say to someone if you knew they were going to die on a certain date? How should that be any different from how you talk to people anyway? What if today was *your* last day? Would you do anything different? Treat your parents with a little more respect? Talk to your little brother a little softer? We should live like we're going to die tomorrow. But remember: We can die knowing that we're going to live forever!

Tuesday

What are you afraid of? Flying? Loud noises? Being made fun of? What really makes you scared? Your fear will tell you a lot about what you believe about God. Because fear and faith cannot be in the same place. It's like light and dark. If you're in a totally

> He will not be afraid of evil tidings; his heart is steadfast, trusting in the LORD.
>
> **Psalm 112:7**

dark room and you turn on the light, the darkness goes away. You can't have both light and dark. Listen, fear and faith can't live together. Let God remove your fear. The next time you get scared, tell God that you trust Him and you want faith. He'll give it to you.

Bring all the tithes into the storehouse.

Malachi 3:10

So how old *do* you have to be to tithe? Does it say tithe when you're 25? Does it say play with your money 'til then, enjoy it while you're young, then once you hit 25 shape up, get straight? No? Well, then that must mean that those verses on tithing are for you, too. When I was younger, my uncle told me to give God 10% of my money every month. He said if you start when you're young, it's easier than trying to start it later. What you do today will determine what you do in the future.

EXTREME FOR JESUS

You younger people, submit yourselves to your elders.
1 Peter 5:5

Can you disobey your teachers just because they aren't Christians? Can you talk bad about the president because he makes laws you don't agree with? Are you ready? The answer is no. Paul tells us that nothing happens without God allowing it, including people being put in authority over you. Now that doesn't mean that you obey earthly authority above God, especially if they ask you to do something immoral. But if what they demand is not against God or His Word, then you have to obey. How have you dishonored someone in authority? How can you change your attitude?

> As we have opportunity, let us
> do good to all.
>
> Galatians 6:10

Daydreaming is a lot of fun. You and your friends start dreaming up all of the ways you can go out and help people. There are a lot of needs, and you all have some free time to give. You start by praying for God to lay on your heart which way will be best for all of you to serve. After three weeks of praying, you talk some more about the possibilities. These weekly meetings go on for about another four weeks, and you come up with several more good ideas. You all decide to pray some more. Two more weeks go by, and others now have some more ideas for discussion. These are all good times of prayer and discussion, but you've missed the opportunity. People across the street still need to hear. Don't just talk about it; do something.

People don't usually like it when someone takes credit for something that someone else did. But guess what! We get to take credit for what Christ did. Because of His death

"Because I live, you will live also."

Joh 14:19

and resurrection, we have power over death, too! By believing that Jesus is the Son of God and that He died for our sins, we can have eternal life. For Christians, death is not the end. It's freedom from our earthly bodies and an awesome opportunity to live in heaven with God. So, have you accepted His offer of eternal life? Do it today and live forever.

"Have I not commanded you? Be strong and of good courage; do not be afraid, nor be dismayed, for the LORD your God is with you wherever you go."

Joshua 1:9

The race was on. To win, Reggie had to clear a 90-foot jump. As he lined up the jump, fear crept in and he hesitated, then he flew full-throttle across the jump. Of the 90 feet, Reg jumped 85 feet. His motorcycle smacked the ground and, like a cannon, shot him over the front. While leaving the hospital with a broken wrist, cut chin, and concussion, Reggie said he knew he failed because he hesitated. What is it that you really want to do when you get out of high school? Ask God for courage. Decide, commit it to Him, and go at it full-on.

Be sober, be vigilant; because your adversary the devil walks about like a roaring lion, seeking whom he may devour.

1 Peter 5:8

Throw a frog in a pot of boiling water and he'll leap out every time. Put him in cold water and slowly heat it; the frog will sit there and boil to death. Continue putting yourself in bad situations, and eventually you won't feel the danger; and before you know it, you'll be in deep trouble. Stay alert. Know that Satan wants you to get used to living outside of God's rules on the little things, then he'll slowly turn up the heat and try to destroy you. What kind of things are you into? Could Satan use them to destroy you?

> **Where sin abounded, grace abounded much more.**
> Romans 5:20

Ever stop hanging with someone because of a fight? They made you so mad you just couldn't be around them? Fights can total a relationship, but they don't have to. Conflict isn't such a bad thing. If you do it right, it can draw you closer to one another. Fight right? How? One word—forgiveness. Let people be different; let them be wrong. If you run away from every relationship that has conflict, you won't have any relationships left. God has forgiven you of all of your wrongs, so how can you not forgive your friend? Thank God for all the stuff He hasn't allowed to total your relationship with Him.

Thursday

In the art of fighting, it's so important that you fight fair. No one likes a cheap fighter—taking potshots at you while you're trying to make a point. Have you ever been interrupted while you were talking? It stinks, huh? The key to good fighting is listening. Let the other person have their say. Don't interrupt them, thinking you know what they're about to say. It shows them no respect and only makes matters worse. The same goes for your relationship with God. Listen to Him. Don't think you know what He is going to say; you don't. Just listen.

> He who answers a matter before he hears it, it is folly and shame to him.
>
> **Proverbs 18:13**

You will guide me with Your counsel.

Psalm 73:24

Ah, yeah. This is the life. You're in your dad's new Mustang convertible, screaming down the road. Since you just went from 0 to 60 in five seconds, you feel like your skin is trying its best to hold on to your bones. Then you think, "This would be even better if I knew how to drive." Well, for some that's life. We're tearing down life's highway, not knowing what to do to stay on track. Introducing "Divine Driver's Ed." God will show you every turn, twist, and even the scenic routes in life's road, if you'll just let Him drive and be open to learn from Him. You'll make mistakes, hit some barriers, flatten some cones, probably stall out, too. Just remember: Let God hold the wheel and you'll enjoy the ride.

EXTREME FOR JESUS

Now to Him who is able to do exceedingly abundantly above all that we ask or think, according to the power that works in us.
Ephesians 3:20

It is straight down. A triple, black-diamond ski run that you and your friend are ready for, but scared to do. What if you fall and break something? What if you lose complete control on the way down? You're filled with lots of "what ifs." As you continue to prepare, you realize that it isn't the run that's making you nervous; it's that you brought your friend skiing so that you could share your faith. Sharing seems so hard that the skiing looks like the "bunny hill" in comparison. You've been flatly rejected every time you've shared your faith, and those past experiences make you want to clam up. Will God get you through both encounters? Will you let Him?

> Through the LORD's mercies we
> are not consumed, because His
> compassions fail not. They are
> new every morning; great is
> Your faithfulness.

Lamentations 3:22-23

Who's the most dependable person you know? Why? People that are dependable are trusted by many and are called on to complete important tasks. Think about it. Would you want someone to handle something very important to you if they weren't dependable? What are the qualities that dependable people have? God meets all of those qualities. God is always there. He keeps His word, and He gets the job done! God is faithful! How has God been faithful to you? Thank Him for His faithfulness today!

"**F**orget it. I'm outta here!" Ever felt like that? Your parents seem so clueless, you would be better off on your own. Hey, they aren't perfect. But they want what's best for you. Remember the guy in this story? He took off and ended up eating pig slop. (And you thought the cafeteria food was bad.) Then he eventually crawled back to his dad. You won't always get along with your parents, but don't run. Get outta their face and cool off. Don't end up eating with the pigs.

"And the younger of them said to his father, 'Father, give me the portion of goods that falls to me.' So he divided to them his livelihood."

Luke 15:12

He who goes about as a talebearer reveals secrets; therefore do not associate with one who flatters with his lips.

Proverbs 20:19

If you have a problem with someone, do you go to them, or do you talk about it to someone else? If you're talking about it to someone else, you're a talebearer—a gossip. Imagine what it would be like if what you were saying was announced over the loudspeaker. Would you be OK with it? Or would you be embarrassed? If you wouldn't want your friend to hear what you're saying about them, then chances are, you shouldn't be saying it.

EXTREME FOR JESUS

> He who has a slack hand becomes poor, but the hand of the diligent makes rich.
>
> ## Proverbs 10:4

It has been said that we are what we do. If that's right, then what are you? A couch potato? An athlete? What do you choose to make a habit? Are you self-controlled? Or do your emotions run your life? If you want to be successful, then you will need to practice sacrificing what you want *now* for what you know you'll want *later.* If you want to get good grades, you might have to sacrifice going to the movies so that you can study. If you want to be a good friend, you will have to practice compromise. If you want to save enough money to buy yourself a car, you might have to do without some other things now. Get the picture?

> "Why do you look at the speck
> in your brother's eye, but do
> not consider the plank in your
> own eye?"

Matthew 7:3

They're the ones who have the issue. As a matter of fact, you can't believe they can even live with themselves. They act as if they're better than anyone else. They never let anyone into their group (of two) and use the guise that they're best friends. They're so exclusive that they won't do anything with anyone else. You make sure that you let everyone around know how wrong these two people are because they won't hang out with anyone else. As a matter of fact, you've made it your personal mission to point out the sin in others, feeling like you're using your gift of discernment. Who really has the issue?

If you work hard in school, you expect to get good grades. If you work hard at your job, you expect a paycheck every couple of weeks. If you break the speed limit, you expect to pay the speeding ticket. If you live a life of sin, there's nothing else that you can expect to earn except death. But Jesus has a deal for you that actually seems too good to be true: Your bill has already been paid on the Cross. There's nothing you can do to clear your record. It's already been done. Accept the gift of eternal life.

> The wages of sin is death, but the gift of God is eternal life in Christ Jesus our Lord.
>
> **Romans 6:23**

Beware lest anyone cheat you through philosophy and empty deceit, according to the tradition of men, according to the basic principles of the world, and not according to Christ.

Colossians 2:8

You're flippin' through the channels; everyone is selling something. Then you land on the video channel. You groove to the music, swearing that you don't listen to the words. You just like the funky beat. They're selling something, too. Sex, drugs, party, sex, gangs, money, sex . . . get the picture? The music is not the enemy. The god of that music is the Enemy. And he'll do whatever he can to sell you his lies. Check what you're watching and listening to. If not, you could start believing the lies.

EXTREME FOR JESUS

> All have sinned and fall
> short of the glory of God.
> **Romans 3:23**

You sneak out Saturday night, take your parents' car, cruise around. . . . Crash! Your parents are upset, but happy you're OK. You tell them you're sorry and you'll never do it again. They forgive you, but there's still a wrecked car. You have to work weekends to make money to pay for the car.

That's kinda like what happens when we sin. God forgives us when we ask Him to, but there are natural consequences that come with our actions—not abuse from God, but natural consequences. If you've sinned, seek and accept God's forgiveness. Then accept the consequences without getting ticked at God. He didn't make the choice. You did.

> "If you ... remember that your brother has something against you ... be reconciled to your brother."
>
> Matthew 5:23-24

Two guys are tossing the football. One throws it hard and spikes the other guy in the head. This guy gets so mad he turns and leaves. The fun is over. Same two guys toss the ball. One throws it, and the other just stands there and lets it drop. The fun is over. When you fight, do you try to hurt the other person, or do you walk away as soon as conflict starts? Both styles end the game. Both ways of handling an argument are not cool. When you have a problem with someone, Jesus asks you to work it out—even if it isn't *your* problem.

Thursday

Can you choose to forgive those who have hurt you? Or do you want to hold on to the hurt? If we continue to dwell on stupid things people have done to us, we're disobeying God. How can you love your enemy, or even your friend, if you keep reliving the pain they've caused? Find the strength to forgive. Pray for them and let God do the rest.

> "Love your enemies, bless those who curse you, do good to those who hate you."
>
> **Matthew 5:44**

> But be doers of the word, and not hearers only.
>
> James 1:22

You and your friends decide that, before you go out for the evening, you'd like to go to the hill with your dad's new four-wheel-drive truck and try it out. The four of you pile into the cab and begin to have the time of your life—until you slide down the hill into a big rut that buries your dad's truck up to its windows in mud. You and your friends crawl out the windows and try to think about what to do. For two hours you talk about all the possible ways to get the truck out. Finally, you grab some shovels and just start digging, knowing that something has to be done. Is your Christian life similar? Do you talk a lot about what you would like to do or should be doing for God? Why don't you just do it?

EXTREME FOR JESUS

Whether we live or die, we are the Lord's.

Romans 14:8

Against your better judgment, you get your class to sit in seats different from your assigned ones—all for the benefit of a good laugh on the substitute as he tries to figure out who's who in the class. Naturally, you get caught, and the next day, when your regular teacher shows up, it is revealed that you were the instigator of the prank. You get detention for the next three days after school, and it's with your teacher, who is not pleased. He tells you that for the next three days he "owns you." One good thing that comes out of it is that his comment gets you to thinking. Who does own you? Who do you belong to? Is it evident in your life who your owner is?

> As many of us as were baptized into Christ Jesus were baptized into His death.

Do you know the difference between a cucumber and a pickle? A cucumber is what you pick from your garden or your grocer's produce shelf. A pickle is a cucumber that's been washed and soaked in a vinegar solution, which permanently changes its characteristics and taste.

"Baptized into Christ" comes from the original Greek word *baptizo,* which means that we're permanently changed. Our relationship with Christ should change us not only on the inside, but on the outside, too. Are you only a cucumber, or have you been "washed and soaked" in Christ's righteousness, permanently changed inwardly to have His sweet taste?

Tuesday

Jesus came to offer us life. The opposite of life, of course, is death. What most people don't realize is that they have a choice between the two. You can choose life by accepting all that God has to offer, including discipline and correction. Or you can choose to reject what God offers, living life your own way—free from any sort of discipline or expectations in your life. You've gotta know, though—rejecting God is the same as choosing your death sentence. The choice is up to you.

> Harsh discipline is for him who forsakes the way, and he who hates correction will die.
>
> **Proverbs 15:10**

> We must give the more earnest heed to the things we have heard, lest we drift away.
>
> Hebrews 2:1

Ever seen those commercials where someone is just drifting out in the ocean? No food. No water. No nothing. Ever felt like that? Separated. Alone. Depressed.

We can drift away from God when we're not anchored in His Word. Even though we may think some things—like prayer, reading the Bible *every* day, checking our attitude—are not that important, they keep us anchored to God. When we don't pray and talk to God and read His Word, we start to drift away from Him and soon find ourselves in a deserted place. Be faithful about the things that may not seem that important or exciting. Challenge yourself to spend time with God through prayer and Bible study every day. You'll find an anchor through even the wildest storms.

EXTREME FOR JESUS

In the multitude of words sin is not lacking, but he who restrains his lips is wise.

Proverbs 10:19

"Johnny, please be quiet." "Johnny, hush." "SHUT-UP!" Know someone that talks too much? Sure. You get around them and *blah, blah, blah.* It's like they don't say anything, but they're always talking. It's annoying, but that's about it. Wrong. The Bible says if someone talks a lot, then their words can push them over the edge into sin. So don't just watch *what* you say, but also watch *how much* you say. Don't let yourself get choked on too many words.

> "Do not lay up for yourselves
> treasures on earth."
>
> Matthew 6:19

What's a two-year-old's favorite word? "Mine." Why is it that from the moment we can talk we want to own things? As we get older, we just seem to want more and more things. Trouble is, the more you own, the more you have to lose. Some people spend a lot of money and energy to protect what they own. When they do lose something or someone, they're destroyed. They hate God; they hate whoever took what was theirs. The thing is that everything and everyone belongs to God. Once we get that down we don't have to worry, because we really possess nothing. Don't hold on too tightly to your stuff.

I borrowed some ballet shoes from a friend, and I keep forgetting to give them back to her. Every time I see her I think about those shoes. When I'm around her, all I think about is how and when I can get them back to her. It's a lot like our debt of love to one another. We need to be like this when we hang out with people throughout our day. We should be thinking about how and when we can pay on our debt of love to them. How will you pay an installment on your debt of love to someone else today?

> Owe no one anything except to love one another.
>
> Romans 13:8

Restore to me the joy of Your salvation.

Psalm 51:12

You're rafting one of the wildest rivers in your area and loving every minute of it. The water is rough and your raft is secure. The floods from the year before have made the river a little different from the other times you've rafted here. All of a sudden you hit a rapid you don't expect, and you fall out of the boat. You get caught underwater, and the people left in the boat are totally worried about your safety. After about five minutes in the water, your friends finally get you back into the boat. Everyone is stoked that you are in and OK. Do we have that same kind of zeal and passion for God? Have you forgotten what it's like to be rescued from the undercurrents of sin? Ask God to restore to you the true joy of His salvation.

EXTREME FOR JESUS

I pour out my complaint before Him; I declare before Him my trouble.

Psalm 142:2

One problem with large corporations can be that the voice of the "little" person never gets heard. Their questions aren't answered, and important issues are not addressed. This usually leaves the employee feeling like they don't matter.

Our relationship with Jesus allows us total access to the One in charge. The awesome thing is this: Not only does God listen to our gripes and complaints, He also knows how to handle them. Cry out to Him. Tell Him what it is that you don't like. He's always ready to listen.

Jesus said to them, "Follow
Me, and I will make you become fishers of men." They
immediately left their nets
and followed Him.

Mark 1:17-18

Road trip. Throw some stuff in the car, pick
up your friends, and go. Don't really know
where. Just go. There's something exciting
about living moment by moment, not knowing
what to expect. Jesus took His disciples on the
ultimate road trip. And you know what is really
wild? They didn't even know Jesus beforehand.
He walked up to these guys, who were usually
at work, and said, "Follow Me." Then He took
off walking. He didn't wait for a response.
These guys had to make a quick decision. Drop
everything and risk it. Or keep doing the same
old thing. Every day when you wake up, Jesus
says to you, "Follow Me." It's your choice. What
are you going to do?

Thursday

Whoever thinks the Christian life is boring is way wrong. When you live every day in the presence of God, your life begins to become a total rush. Jesus planned it this way. He didn't come down here to give you a wimpy, little, fearful life where you have to hide behind

> "I have come that they may have life, and that they may have it more abundantly."
>
> John 10:10

your Bible in order to be safe from the big, bad world. No. He offers a life of adventure. A life so full of passion and excitement that nothing on earth could replace it. So don't expect God to be boring. Expect Him to be extreme. Expect an adventure. Expect life to the fullest.

> "You shall not hate your brother in your heart."
>
> Leviticus 19:17

Brothers and sisters can really get on your nerves. Sometimes you just want to smack them. God knows that. That's why He told the Jews not to even hate them in their hearts. If it weren't an issue, He wouldn't have had to put it in the law. But it is. Your brothers and sisters by blood or in Christ are totally loved by God—even if they sometimes are spastic. Try to see them the way God sees them. Love them the way He loves them. In the end, you'll have a really good friend who will stand by you forever.

EXTREME FOR JESUS

LORD, who may abide in Your tabernacle? . . . He who swears to his own hurt and does not change.
Psalm 15:1, 4

Your parents ask you to be home right after school so you can take your little brother to his dentist appointment. Mom has to sign some important papers at the bank, and she's counting on you. There's no problem or conflict. At lunch all your friends decide it would be cool to go water skiing as soon as school gets out. You'll be the one driving the boat. The thought of your brother's appointment never enters your mind. You go to the lake, and mom misses her bank meeting to take your brother to the dentist. It was an honest oversight, right? But to your parents, you've let them down. Once your integrity is lost, it's hard to gain it back. Are you a person of your word?

"He who believes in Me . . . out of his heart will flow rivers of living water."

John 7:38

There's a body of water in Israel called the Dead Sea. It's "dead" because nothing lives in it. "Why?" you may ask. Because the water is completely stagnant. See, there are no outlets for the water. It just sits there—dead, dirty. Our Christian lives can easily become like the Dead Sea if we don't have outlets for our faith—sharing Christ and giving our lives to others. It's easy for us to become stagnant and lifeless. Is your Christian walk a fountain of life or a Dead Sea? What things have you done this past week to let the living waters of God's love flow through you to others?

In the days of the Roman army, soldiers would shoot fiery arrows dipped in tar at the shields of their enemies. When the arrows hit the shields, the flaming tar would splatter on them. Those that were experienced in battle knew that all the enemy was trying to do was to get them to throw down their shields. That would make them easier targets.

> Above all, taking the shield of faith with which you will be able to quench all the fiery darts of the wicked one.
>
> **Ephesians 6:16**

Let's face it. You're in a battle. And Satan wants to take you out permanently. With God's help you can hold on to your shield. Don't let go of your faith. Satan knows that as long as you have that protection, he can't touch you. Hang in there. You don't have to fear the Enemy. Because of your faith in God, he fears you more.

When they saw the boldness of Peter and John, and perceived that they were uneducated and untrained men, they marveled. And they realized that they had been with Jesus.

Acts 4:13

Have you ever picked up your drink on a hot day, ready to taste the fruit punch? You take a big gulp and . . . iced tea! It feels like your face is turning inside out. Your tongue runs and hides. You were ready for one thing and got another. Shock to the system.

That's what happens with us as Christians. The world around us is expecting us to act like them. Then shocker . . . we're acting like Christ! We've been called to walk different; talk, act, and be different. This won't always be easy or win a lot of fans because we're not what the world expects. Be bold. Take a stand. Be different for Christ.

EXTREME FOR JESUS

God did not spare the angels who sinned, but cast them down to hell and delivered them into chains of darkness, to be reserved for judgment.

2 Peter 2:4

Would a loving God really send someone to hell? God *is* a loving God. He offers love to everyone who accepts Him. But God is also just and holy. Because of that, He must judge sin. Those who do not repent of their sins and accept His offer of salvation will not be able to escape His final verdict of eternal death. God's gift of life would have no value without the threat of death. So the choice is yours. Will you choose life or death?

> Count it all joy when you fall
> into various trials, knowing
> that the testing of your faith
> produces patience.
>
> James 1:2-3

Do you like tests? Why not? They're usually hard to get through, aren't they? Especially if you aren't prepared for them. The Bible talks about the testing of our faith as if it's a guarantee. There's no way to escape tests because they're there to strengthen you in the subject of God. So would it help if I gave you the answer to the questions? Stand and trust. Stand means don't run off in fear or anger. Trust means knowing God will use whatever you're going through for your good. That's it. So your parents divorce. Stand and trust. Your crush called it off. Stand and trust. Your friend is killed. Stand and trust. God is faithful.

Weekend

Basketball has always been a passion of yours. You play by the hours in your driveway and at the local playground. Yet you have never played for an organized team. "Too much politics" has always been what you thought, and you've even told people that the politics keep you away. Now as you get into

> "No one, having put his hand to the plow, and looking back, is fit for the kingdom of God."
>
> Luke 9:62

high school, you think you might like to at least try out. You're pretty sure you'll make the team, but what if you don't. Could you live with being cut? The agony of the decision is intense. You don't know what to do, and you never will until you take a risk and try. Do you live your life by the "what ifs," or can you try living with no regrets?

Fear not, for I am with you; be not dismayed, for I am your God. I will strengthen you, yes, I will help you.

Isaiah 41:10

It's going to be what you envision as the hardest thing you've ever done in your life—going to your grandma's funeral. Your imagination is getting the best of you, and the sense of dread is slowly creeping in. You want to be there for your mom, because you know she needs you right now. You're dealing with your own sense of loss as well, because you and Grandma were very close. During the most awkward and difficult circumstances is the time when God steps up. He'll always be there for you, and better still . . . He *wants* to be there. The question is, are you going to let Him or try to go it alone?

Walk in the Spirit, and you shall not fulfill the lust of the flesh.

Galatians 5:16

There are two forces at war within us—our flesh and the Spirit of God. Our flesh is fueled by our emotions; we go after what we think will make us feel good. Focusing on feelings and emotions will give us temporary satisfaction. But remember: It *is* only temporary. Contrary to our emotions is God's Spirit, who works to help us do what's right and good. When we ask the Spirit of God to direct our lives, we can live in a place of joy, peace, and happiness. Don't rely on how you feel to determine what you believe. Know what you believe, and let that determine how you feel.

EXTREME FOR JESUS

Sing praises to God, sing
praises! Sing praises to our
King, sing praises!

`Psalm 47:6`

There you are, sitting in church. They're
singing songs. You're just kinda mumbling
the words, not really thinking about them.
That's not your thing. You don't get a lot out of
singing these praise songs. Exactly. They're not
for you. They're for God. Everything else in the
service is for you. Do you think God ever sat up
and said, "Wow, that's a good point pastor; I
never thought about that!"? No. See, singing
praises to God is totally for Him. He loves to
hear you—no matter what you think your voice
is like. That part of the service is all about
showing God how much you love Him. So next
time, don't be shy. Sing to Him, think about the
words, and love the Savior.

Have you ever had to chase somebody? You totally liked them, but they were hard to get. But once they liked you things were great. There's something to be said about the chase. Anything we get too easily doesn't hold much value after awhile.

> Flee sexual immorality.
> 1 Corinthians 6:18

God has put a price on sex. Marriage is the price. If you get sex too easily, then look out. Soon it will be worth nothing. Don't let anybody fool you into thinking it's OK outside of marriage. God has given it a high price.

We do not look at the things which are seen, but at the things which are not seen. For the things which are seen are temporary, but the things which are not seen are eternal.

2 Corinthians 4:18

Practice looking through things. Look through the obvious to the unobvious, the unseen. God's fingerprints are everywhere, but you really have to look. How? By concentrating on the eternal things. Things God has given us, like Jesus, the Holy Spirit, worship, and fellowship. Then you get used to seeing what most people can't see. You get used to seeing God in stuff, even in the bad stuff. Practice ignoring the temporary by concentrating on the eternal. Life will be a whole lot easier.

EXTREME FOR JESUS

"Give to Your servant an understanding heart to judge Your people, that I may discern between good and evil."
1 Kings 3:9

Can you only imagine what was going through Solomon's mind when God told him to ask for whatever he wanted. You think of all that you could have with that one little granted wish. Solomon asked only for "an understanding heart." Realize that you can have all the right clothes, the right friends, the right car, even the perfect family, but if you're a jerk, it doesn't matter. Solomon wanted God to make him a special person on the inside. Maybe he was hoping God would also take care of the external issues. God did take care of the outside, even though Solomon didn't ask for it. Are you striving for external glory or internal security?

> Abram said to Lot, "Please let
> there be no strife between you
> and me, and between my
> herdsmen and your herdsmen;
> for we are brethren."

Genesis 13:8

Look around the dentist's office and you will see a poster with nasty looking teeth and the caption, "Only floss the ones you want to keep." It's amazing how a little bit of stuff left between teeth can destroy the whole tooth. This is the same way with our relationships. Sometimes we get our feelings hurt, or someone makes us mad, and we just let it sit there. We don't clean out the resentment. This tiny stuff, left unresolved, will destroy your relationship. The next time you have a problem with a friend, talk with them. Work it out, or it could totally destroy your friendship.

You have a choice about who is going to be your enemy. "But you don't know how they're treating me," you might be saying. Sure, people can be pretty mean sometimes. But your choice in

He who covers a transgression seeks love.

Proverbs 17:9

the matter is how you're going to let another person's behavior affect you. You may be justified in your anger or frustration. But the only way to come out ahead is by showing grace and mercy toward the other person—yes, even toward one who has dissed you. Get rid of your enemies by showing them love, even when they don't deserve it.

Joshua said to them, "Do not be afraid, nor be dismayed; be strong and of good courage, for thus the LORD will do to all your enemies against whom you fight."

Joshua 10:25

The stories in the Old Testament talk a lot about war and battle. This verse tells us that God can be trusted to do whatever He needs to do to bring victory. Do you sometimes feel like you're going through a kind of "battle"? God wants you to know that He's right there going through it with you. He's making sure that you get the victory. Battle and conflict are never easy. But you can have confidence that God is going ahead of you, clearing the path to get you to the other side.

EXTREME FOR JESUS

> "You meant evil against me; but God meant it for good."
> ### Genesis 50:20

His brothers were so sick of him being daddy's boy. They hated him. So they turned him over to some strangers who made him a slave. They told their daddy that he was killed by a wild animal. So no one looked for him. How could he go on living knowing how bad his brothers had treated him? How could he live as a slave, as a prisoner, as a servant and not be totally ticked off at his family? He could because he believed God was in control. Even in the midst of all the stupid stuff, God was in control.

> "In the world you will have tribulation; but be of good cheer, I have overcome the world."
>
> John 16:33

The kids whose friends were shot in the school shootings have two options. They can blame God for it and be depressed and destroyed by the event. Or they can choose happiness. Huh? Happiness? How could they be happy? Well, if this verse is true—and it is—then that's what Jesus offers us. He never said there wouldn't be traumas. They're the result of sin. But He did say you have a choice in how you respond to the traumas: to feel bummed or to be of good cheer. Choose for yourself. Will you let life get you down, or will you say, "He has overcome the world!"?

Bumblebees can't fly. Physicists say a bee's body is just too big for the size of its wings. But nobody ever told the bees this, so they go ahead and fly anyway. How many things have we been told we can't do? How many things have we told our-selves we can't do? The truth is: All things are possible in Christ—even the things that seem impossible to us. Maybe we shouldn't ask our-selves, "Can I do this?" but, "Can God do this?"

> "With men this is impossible, but with God all things are possible."
>
> Matthew 19:26